The Empress

Tanika Gupta was born in London the year after her parents arrived from Calcutta. Over twenty five years, she has written over twenty five plays that have been produced in major theatres across the UK. She has written thirty radio plays for the BBC and several original television dramas, as well as scripts for *EastEnders*, *Grange Hill* and *The Bill*. She has taught drama and run workshops in South Africa, Australia, New Zealand, Cuba, India, the USA, the Netherlands, Germany, Argentina, Chile and across the UK. She is a fellow of Rose Bruford College, runs courses for the Arvon Foundation and has led playwriting workshops in many UK universities, as well as for the National Theatre, the Royal Court, Hampstead Theatre, the Young Vic and Theatre Royal Stratford East. She has been writer-in-residence at the National Theatre and Soho Theatre, a fellow at the Playwrights' Studio in Glasgow and a writing tutor in HMP Winchester. She has won numerous awards for her work She was awarded an MBE for her contribution to the Arts in 2009, is a Fellow at Rose Bruford and Royal Central School of Speech and Drama and has an Honorary Doctorate in the Arts from Chichester University.

Jane Garnett has been Fellow and Tutor in History at Wadham College, Oxford since 1987. She has published widely on the religious, intellectual, cultural, gender and art history of the seventeenth to twenty-first centuries. Her book (co-authored with Gervase Rosser), *Spectacular Miracles: transforming images in Italy from the Renaissance to the present* (Reaktion, 2013) was jointly awarded the 2014 ACE/Mercers' International Book Award 'for a book which makes an outstanding contribution to the dialogue between religious faith and the visual arts'. From 1993 to 2004 she was Consultant Editor for Women on the *Oxford Dictionary of National Biography*. From 2011 to 2015 she participated in a major collaborative and interdisciplinary Leverhulme-funded project on the impact of diasporas, within which her focus was on Jewish, Christian and Muslim cultures in East London since 1880. In 2014-15 she co-organized an exhibition and co-edited (with Sunil Shah) *Doh Mix Meh Up: Diaspora and Identity in Art*. She is currently co-director of the Intersectional Humanities Programme in Oxford.

The Empress

TANIKA GUPTA

With commentary and notes by

JANE GARNETT

Series Editors: Sara Freeman, Jenny Stevens,
Chris Megson and Matthew Nichols

methuen | drama

LONDON • NEW YORK • OXFORD • NEW DELHI • SYDNEY

METHUEN DRAMA
Bloomsbury Publishing Plc
50 Bedford Square, London, WC1B 3DP, UK
1385 Broadway, New York, NY 10018, USA
29 Earlsfort Terrace, Dublin 2, Ireland

BLOOMSBURY, METHUEN DRAMA and the Methuen Drama logo are trademarks
of Bloomsbury Publishing Plc

First published in Great Britain by Oberon Books 2013
This edition first published by Methuen Drama 2022
Reprinted 2022 (three times)

Cover design: Ben Anslow
Cover image: An Indian Ayah with two children (© The Picture Art
Collection / Alamy Stock Photo)

A catalogue record for this book is available from the British Library.

A catalog record for this book is available from the Library of Congress.

ISBN: PB: 978-1-3501-9057-3
       ePDF: 978-1-3501-9058-0
       eBook: 978-1-3501-9059-7

Series: Student Editions

Typeset by RefineCatch Limited, Bungay, Suffolk
Printed and bound in Great Britain

To find out more about our authors and books visit www.bloomsbury.com
and sign up for our newsletters.

Contents

Chronology

1963   Tanika Gupta is born on 1 December 1963 in Chiswick, England, to immigrants from Calcutta, India.

1988   Gupta marries David Archer, an anti-poverty activist, whom she met at university.

1991   Gupta is a finalist at the 1991 BBC Young Playwrights festival.

1995   After graduating from Oxford University with a Modern History degree, Gupta begins writing in her spare time. The first professional live performance of a play by Gupta, *Voices on the Wind*, is put on at the National Theatre Studio.

1996   Gupta becomes a full-time writer, having previously worked at an Asian women's refuge in Manchester and as a community worker in Islington.

1996   Gupta's play *Skeleton* is commissioned by the Soho Theatre Company, and Gupta becomes the writer-in-residence of the Soho Theatre.

1997   Gupta breaks into writing for television, authoring multiple episodes for the long-running TV soap operas *EastEnders*, *The Bill* and *Grange Hill* over the next few years.

2000   Gupta's play *The Waiting Room*, which explores ideas of the afterlife, is produced at the National Theatre to critical and commercial acclaim, winning Gupta the 2000 John Whiting Award.

2002   Gupta's play *Sanctuary*, which investigates ideas of place and morality, opens at the Lyttleton Loft, as part of the National Theatre's 'Transformation' season.

2003   Gupta wins the 2003 Asian Women of Achievement Award in the Arts category.

2003   Gupta adapts Harold Brighouse's 1916 comedy *Hobson's Choice*, reimagining the play set within the modern-day Salford Asian community. This production opened at London's Young Vic to critical acclaim, earning Gupta an Olivier Award nomination.

2005   Gupta's play *Gladiator Games* premieres at the Sheffield Crucible Theatre, before transferring to Theatre Royal Stratford East. The show catalogues the incompetence of the official response to Zahid Mubarek's murder while he was in prison. Gupta has indicated that this is the play she is most proud of.

2006   Gupta's play *Sugar Mummies* opens at the Royal Court, exploring female sex tourism in the Caribbean.

2008   Gupta is appointed a Member of the Order of the British Empire (MBE) in the New Year Honours for her services to drama.

2008   Gupta's comedy *Meet the Mukherjees* premieres at the Bolton Octagon Theatre, exploring the prejudices and fears felt when minority families are joined together through marriage.

2010   Mohammed Abdul Karim's surviving family, who emigrated to Pakistan during the Partition, reveals his private diary and some of his correspondences with Queen Victoria, which they had previously hidden.

2012   Gupta adapts Henrik Ibsen's *A Doll's House* for BBC Radio 3, transposing the setting to 1879 India, where Nora (renamed 'Niru') is an Indian woman married to Torvald (renamed 'Tom'), an English man working for the British colonial administration in Calcutta. This production For Best adaptation BBC Audio Drama Award for Best Adaptation.

2013   Gupta's *The Empress* is first performed at the Swan Theatre, Stratford-upon-Avon, directed by Emma Rice, the Artistic Director of Kneehigh.

2016   Gupta is made a fellow of the Royal Society of Literature.

2017   *Lions and Tigers* is produced at the Globe.

2021   Gupta's new monologue *The Overseas Student*, which explores an eighteen-year-old Gandhi's education in London, premieres as part of the Lyric Hammersmith's *Out West* programme, featuring alongside work by Simon Stephens and Roy Williams.

Introduction

It all begins with a good story. Or, in this case, three. *The Empress* has a strong dramatic shape, structured around two parallel love stories: one based on Queen Victoria's controversial relationship with her Indian servant, the other between a sailor (lascar) and a nursemaid (ayah) travelling to Britain from India in 1887 – the year of the Queen's Golden Jubilee. The action cuts between the ship (and its destination in the east London docks) and different royal residences. Also on the ship are Dadabhai Naoroji, from 1892 to 1895 Liberal MP for Finsbury Central in London, as well as co-founder (in 1885) of the Indian National Congress, and the eighteen-year-old Gandhi. Private romance is mapped onto world history.

The main characters are both historical and fictional. The dialogue is of course all fictional, but grounded in historical understanding and plausibility. The core character in many respects is Rani, the young nursemaid/ayah, whose name means queen in Hindi, and whom her lover, Hari, describes as his empress. She longs to meet Queen Victoria, and – whilst this never happens – the setting of their stories in conversation for the audience forms the spine of the play. Lascar Sally, the boarding-house keeper, and Firoza, the older ayah, represent female solidarity in the face of adversity. The dashing of Rani's dreams and illusions of what London would represent was substituted for by the opening up of different opportunities and hopes. The characterization of the different Indian men – Hari, the low-class/-caste lascar; Abdul Karim, who cultivates an air of superiority; the young Gandhi, thinking of how to become an English gentleman; and the more experienced Dadabhai – opens up both further dimensions of human drama and insight into the variegated forms of engagement with the Empire.

All the characters are constrained by their social situation – the Queen Empress no less than her subjects – and the play explores the human complexities involved. It breaks down a simple picture of the British Empire, and opens up lively debate about intersections between ethnicity, class (and caste), gender and religion. It underlines how well established and socially diverse was the Asian presence in Britain in the nineteenth century: British Asian history did not begin after the Second World War. It is a long, rich and embedded culture. The play was topical and empowering when it was first performed by the Royal Shakespeare Company at Stratford-upon-Avon in the spring of 2013. In many ways, it seems even more so as I write now in 2021.

The Playwright

Tanika Gupta was brought up – first in Hastings, then in north London – in a Bengali family with deep roots in Indian poetry, theatre and dance. In 1965 her parents – Gairika and Tapan Gupta – had founded The Tagoreans as a vehicle for promoting the poetry and philosophy of the hugely important writer and thinker Rabindranath Tagore, and as a child Tanika performed alongside them in Tagorean dance-dramas. She was encouraged to go on regular 'de-Anglicization' trips to Kolkata (Calcutta), so as to educate herself about where her family had come from. Her great-uncle was the revolutionary anti-imperialist Dinesh Gupta, who was hanged in 1931 for an attack on the Writers' Building in central Calcutta/Kolkata. Her play *Lions and Tigers*, written for and performed at the Sam Wanamaker Playhouse in London in 2017 on the seventieth anniversary of Indian independence, drew on his eloquent letters to his family from prison to complicate one-dimensional projections of heroism or martyrdom and explore the political through personal experience. She won the James Tait Black Award in 2018 for this play.

Researching and writing *The Empress* looked through the other end of the telescope. It was for her a voyage of discovery about the late-nineteenth-century history of South Asians in London. She says that when she is beginning to think about writing a play, the story always comes first. She had grown up hearing her father tell stories drawn from Hindu tradition and Indian folk culture, and had absorbed the rhythms and images of that storytelling. Ironically, though, she knew very little of the histories – the stories – of Asians in Britain. The play became a very personal project, a rewriting of history. Strongly critical of the structures of imperial power, she yet sees the play as a celebration of relationships between the British and people from the Indian subcontinent, who interacted in so many different ways both in India and in Britain. Personal relationships are always messy and entangled. Drama – whether on the page or in performance – gives us ways to work through the challenges of our own lives through engagement with those of others. Tanika Gupta's plays have addressed with intelligence and sensitivity the cross-cultural dimensions of this process. Having a strong historical sensibility, she brings out the particularities of time and place and social perspective, whilst always finding vivid points of affinity. By directing the imaginative lens from new angles, she challenges stereotypes and provokes deeper reflection – in the process also making the story more engaging.

As well as being steeped in Indian classics, from childhood she read the great storytellers of the Western canon – the writers who have traditionally been regarded as fundamental elements of a shared literary and cultural tradition. She has written several plays which transpose iconic nineteenth-century novels or plays into an Indian context. The effect is not just to show that the narrative can travel and connect with a new audience, but to reignite its politics and its impact through the process of de-familiarization and re-connection. Her version of Charles Dickens's *Great Expectations* (premiered in Watford in 2010) was set in the India of 1861. Focusing on the encouragement to educated Indians to aspire to become English gentlemen, she illuminated the ways in which the disillusionments so often experienced in the process had the effect of enabling people to understand better their identity and status as Indians. This was true of Pip in her adaptation of Dickens's novel as it was true of Gandhi in *The Empress*. Coming to England to study law, French and ballroom dancing, Gandhi found himself reading the *Bhagavad Gita* for the first time together with two Jewish men in east London. As she highlights in her Gandhi monologue first performed in 2021 at the Lyric Hammersmith, Gandhi's visits to London were fundamental to his realizing himself as Indian. Meanwhile, the figure of Miss Havisham (modelled on a real-life story of a woman in Australia who was jilted at the altar and died thirty years later still wearing her wedding dress) reminded Gupta of elderly relics of the Raj who had stayed on in Calcutta/Kolkata after Partition and had metaphorically stopped the clock in order to block out the realities of the post-colonial world. Most of all, she thought of her twenty-four-year-old father, who had sailed from Bombay to London in 1961 with a one-pound note in his pocket, hoping to find fame and fortune. Great expectations.

Tanika Gupta's re-imagining of Henrik Ibsen's 1879 play *A Doll's House* (which won the BBC Audio Drama Award in 2013) was put on to great acclaim at the Lyric Hammersmith as the opening play of Rachel O'Riordan's first season as artistic director in 2019. Set in Calcutta/Kolkata in the same year that Ibsen wrote the play (and shortly after Queen Victoria had been made Empress of India in 1877), its interleaving of gender, class, ethnicity and racialization made a powerful impact, sharpening even more forcefully the psychological drama of the original. Nora – now Niru – is an Indian married to a colonial British chief of tax collection, who sees himself as liberal in politics and gender attitudes, not least for having married her, yet patronisingly exoticizes her as his 'Indian princess' or 'little chirruping Indian skylark'. As a Christian convert who wears a sari, she is marginalized both by British colonial wives and other Indian women. Her personal transition from dependent plaything to independent voice challenges brutal assertions of racial superiority as well as patriarchy.

Contexts for *The Empress*

Early twenty-first-century global and national politics

Tanika Gupta started her professional career as a social and community worker, and a comparable commitment to the building of relationships and to challenging the oversimplifications of identity politics drives her plays. She herself has never wanted to be defined as an 'Asian' writer, nor to write plays which only focus on Asian characters. That would imply that all 'Asians' thought the same way, and/or that only 'Asians' could write about or speak for 'their community', which would be a drastic betrayal of the complexities of identity. In 2007 she wrote *White Boy*, in the wake of the murder of a sixteen-year-old boy at her daughters' school. In an interview with the *Evening Standard* on 7 August of that year, she commented:

> We still tend to have Asian plays or black plays or white
> plays. That world of the Tube, where you sit and look around
> you and see all those amazing faces, isn't depicted enough.

She also observed that 'you can't really *be* racist when you have 23 languages in the same class'. Clearly you could – and can – but her point was that it shouldn't be possible. Over the last fifteen to twenty years, Gupta's plays have had to respond to an ever-heightened challenge to the cultivation of a politics of generosity, translation, conversation and trust. Over that period, the global intensification of populist politics has boosted racism and religious prejudice, creating and feeding off paranoia about difference. Islamophobia has increased since 9/11 (the attacks on the World Trade Center in New York on 11 September 2001). Simplified and polarized arguments have distorted debates in Britain about the country's relationship with Europe (especially after the 2016 Brexit referendum) and about immigration as a whole. The language and policy of the 'hostile environment', generated by the Home Office from 2012, and the revelations from 2017/18 of the illegal challenges to the rights and status of the 'Windrush generation' – those who had migrated to Britain from Commonwealth countries before 1973 – have only furthered this destructive tendency and have created a far wider sense of insecurity.

Tanika Gupta's principled and eloquent resistance to such political developments, and her belief in the power of theatre both to enact and to negotiate difference, whilst perhaps over-optimistic, are inspiring. Indeed, the inspiration almost certainly requires the optimism.

Early twenty-first-century theatre: translation and representation

The Empress was premiered at Stratford-upon-Avon in the midst of an important but controversial period for the Royal Shakespeare Company. Its theatres had reopened in 2010 after a major refurbishment project. In 2011, it celebrated its fiftieth anniversary as a theatre company. In 2012, in conjunction with London's hosting of the Olympics, it organized a 'World Shakespeare Festival' involving theatre companies from all over the world performing their own productions of Shakespeare plays (in a variety of languages) in venues across the UK. Its 2012–13 season featured a programme at the Swan Theatre under the headline of 'A World Elsewhere', intended to explore what was going on theatrically in other cultures at the same time as Shakespeare was writing. And it launched touring and educational partnerships with five regional theatres. As a high-profile company, in receipt of significant amounts of public money, it was both keen and under pressure to diversify its casts and its audiences. Its special responsibility for Shakespeare and its home in Stratford-upon-Avon, with its predominantly white, middle-class demographic, are not easy starting-points for a policy of meaningful diversification. But its status and resources mean that it can expand its repertoire beyond Shakespeare and also commission new plays.

The real challenge has been to disentangle different concerns, whilst keeping a critical focus on their interrelationships. What is the interplay between the ethnicity, gender, sexuality, religious culture and generational make-up of audiences? To what extent does the ability to draw in new audiences depend on some sort of cultural identification? If it does, is that a question of authorship, theme, staging or casting? But are there not different forms of identity and cultural affinity, which may in fact cross-connect in usually complex and sometimes unexpected ways? The concept of intersectionality is helpful here. First coined in 1989 by the Black American law professor, feminist and critical race theorist Kimberlé Crenshaw to draw attention to the overlaps and interconnections between social categorizations (racialization, ethnicity, class, gender, religion, etc.) in the workings of power and the framing of discrimination, it provides an important lens for identifying and challenging structural inequities. Moreover, can there not be creative stimulation in strangeness? Should plays in fact set up challenges to audiences' assumptions, potentially making them uncomfortable, rather than risking the feeding of complacency? All these questions complicate strategies around the choice of plays, casting and direction. Claims to 'authenticity' can have the unintended effect of limiting available roles, and also set up the wrong expectations in audiences. Superficial diversification can lead to the reinforcement of stereotypes: casting people of colour as servants, or as exotic or supernatural figures, like the witches in Shakespeare's *Macbeth*. Might there be circumstances in which colour-conscious or gender-conscious casting are more appropriate than a claim to colour- or gender-blindness? Such consciousness (relevant also to the commissioning of new plays) involves consideration of ethnicity and gender as intrinsic to the specific concept of the production, as part of a thought-through interpretative approach. In a society which is neither gender- nor colour-blind, this can be crucial.

In 2013 controversy in this respect was provoked not by *The Empress*, but by the RSC's production of *The Orphan of Zhao* as part of the 'A World Elsewhere' programme. A medieval Chinese play, with unfamiliar, highly stylized and non-naturalistic theatrical conventions, presented fundamental challenges for any audience in modern Britain. It was in fact not a translation as such, but an adaptation by the distinguished British poet James Fenton. For this very reason, it was billed as a deliberately intercultural project. What caused criticism was the apparent mismatch between the fact that only three of the seventeen roles were played by East Asian actors (and those roles in turn unfortunately seemed to reinforce racial stereotyping), and the publicity for the play, much of which was in Mandarin and appealed directly to a British Chinese constituency. The evident confusion of purpose was the problem. Good theatre generates a range of response, and the opening up of cultural consciousness is not the property of any one group. Tanika Gupta has said that she was pleased by how many white British people of an older generation came up to her after performances of *The Empress* to say how much they had learnt. Her play, which – in a naturalistic idiom – deals with relationships within and between cultures in a specific historical moment, foregrounds for the audience the working through of the familiar and the unfamiliar, the expected and the unexpected, in order to reflect on the nature of historical change. It is explicitly a play about history. Even more importantly, it is a play about the act of thinking historically. The point being made is that this way of thinking is as significant for approaching the present and future as for understanding the past.

Victorian worlds: 1887–1901

The Empress is set in the last fourteen years of Queen Victoria's reign. Its cross-cutting between three narratives, the threads of which sometimes interweave and often hang in parallel to each other, points both to the richness of the social tapestry and to the holes, dropped stitches and knots, which make the texture of this tapestry less smooth and legible. The action is staged in several zones of encounter – and non-encounter.

Ayahs and Lascars: ships and docks

The great ships which travelled round the Empire were mobile worlds. On them, some were encouraged to interact; others were kept apart. Their internal arrangements were a microcosm of a socially layered culture, which was even more regulated and controlled on sea than on land. Ayahs like Rani enacted their marginal and transient status by having 'deck-class' tickets, and often had to carry their rolled-up mattresses around with them during the day. They were only permitted to access the cabins of their employers when they were involved in looking after the children they were caring for. They had often built up an extremely close relationship with these children. Yet the voyage to Britain could be the prelude to being dismissed. Ayahs – whether Indian or African – were considered to be very suitable carers for young children, because of stereotyped assumptions about their 'natural' warmth, simplicity and docility. Such qualities were then seen by white British families to disqualify ayahs from contact with children above a certain age, who needed to be socialized and educated by British nannies and governesses, or to go to boarding school in Britain (with the consequence that they were separated from their parents for long periods). The psychological and emotional impact on children (as well as their parents) of this rupture of relationships was considerable, and is seen in a distorted form in the memories of his ayah expressed by Rani's sexually abusive employer. Tellingly, as well as remembering her cooking, he recalls her by name. On ships' passenger lists ayahs were usually simply described by their employer's name (whilst white British servants who travelled in cabin class were listed by their own name). This treatment of them as anonymous and as possessions of the families for whom they worked made it potentially easier to exploit them. In the play, Lord John Oakham remembers the happy parts of his childhood through associating Rani with Jamila, his ayah; the psycho-sexual consequence of this is his seduction and then heartless repulsion of Rani when she becomes pregnant with his child.

The late nineteenth century saw an unprecedented sea traffic to and fro from different parts of the Empire to London and between imperial locations. The opening of the Suez Canal in 1869 made the eastward journey to India easier, and the encouragement to the settlement of white British families in India (and elsewhere) meant that there was increased demand for different sorts of labour on board ship. The origins of the Clan Line, referred to in the opening lascars' song in *The Empress*, lay in a company set up in Liverpool in 1877 to serve the route to Bombay/Mumbai. It became the Clan Line in 1881, following a merger with a Scottish firm, and through various further expansions extended its routes to South Africa, the Persian Gulf and North America. The ocean liner RMS *Empress of India* – the first of many ships named 'Empress', and launched from Barrow-in-Furness in 1891 – was commissioned by the Canadian Pacific Steamship Company to cover the transpacific route between the west coast of Canada and the Far East. Ayahs, as a transnational female labour force, worked not just on the Britain–India route, but hired themselves out as temporary nursemaids to families travelling between different destinations. Their skills and responsibility meant that they could negotiate relatively decent wages. This was not true for lascars. Whilst seamen from all over the world were recruited – especially from Africa, the Caribbean and India – lower-class/caste lascars from India and Ceylon (mostly Muslims) by 1914 constituted 17.5 per cent of the sailors on British-registered ships. They were generally employed for stoking the coal on steamships, and received the lowest wages. In addition, their mobility was particularly tightly regulated. In principle, they could only be discharged in India, although the sick or injured were often left behind, and many jumped ship, and settled in Britain, sometimes taking up with white women who were running boarding houses in the streets around the docks (such as 'Lascar Sally' – and 'Canton Kitty' – whose names identified the ethnicity of their partners), and learning different trades. Some, like Hari, got caught, and were then subjected to even more punitive conditions.

Both lascars and ayahs were potentially vulnerable when they were between periods of employment. Different solidarities – formal and informal – formed in response. And resourcefulness and capacity for survival were evident: one ayah, Mrs Antony Pareira, claimed to have travelled fifty-four times between India and Britain, offering her labour simply for the voyage. Some ayahs, like Rani in the play, managed to use education to get access to a different type of job. Younger ayahs could be advized by more experienced ones, as in the case of Rani and Firoza. There are fleeting traces in the legal records in the 1890s of ayahs successfully taking defaulting employers or keepers of boarding houses to court, sometimes accompanied by fellow ayahs to lend support.

In 1857 – the same year as the Indian Rebellion, which led to the tightening and extension of formal British imperial rule over India – Christian missionaries set up in Limehouse in east London the Strangers' Home for Asiatics, Africans and South Sea Islanders. The idea was that it should be a more morally disciplined alternative to the private lodgings which already existed. In 1900 the London City Mission also took over the Ayahs' Home in Hackney, which it is possible had originally been established in Aldgate in 1825. Both establishments provided subsidized lodging and meals, as well as helping with finding employment and the negotiation of relationships with employers. It is too easy to see these spaces simplistically as contexts of colonial oppression. In fact, whilst of course the unequal power dynamic remained, they did provide scope for respectful cross-faith and transnational encounters. Although they were framed in a Christian form, and provided Christian teaching, they also provided prayer-spaces for Muslims and Hindus, followed dietary principles and offered language instruction. Many South Asians had already come across mission schools in India, and for some conversion was attractive as a means of integration. But it was reported that few in fact did convert. An 'Asiatic Rest' was set up, incorporating an 'oriental' library on Sundays and on weekday evenings. It was said that people came there to see the Qu'ran or pictures of Medina or Mecca. Muslim funerals were facilitated and accompanied; a homesick Hindu young woman with three children in India was helped to get home. In 1882 the Strangers' Home supported lascars who refused to take jobs on warships which were being sent to attack fellow Muslims in Egypt.

It would be equally easy to over-romanticize these points of inter-faith connection, but it is important to acknowledge their existence as markers of the complexity of colonial culture. Moreover, this religious complexity was a practical reality which needed to be addressed. Late-Victorian missionaries and philanthropists, who embodied and identified with Britain's status as a Christian nation and imperial power, saw that any disrespectful treatment of strangers and failure to offer hospitality could undermine both national morality and the impression given of British values. In turn, this would harm the credibility of British rule. A hint of this is given (in Act One, Scene Six) when Rani says: 'In my village, guests are treated as gods.'

The Queen Empress

Victoria had become Queen in 1837. On 1 January 1877, she was proclaimed Empress of India at a spectacular ceremony in Delhi. To celebrate the Golden Jubilee of her accession to the throne in 1887, the Governor of the North-West Frontier in India sent her two manservants as a present – these men of another race being treated simply as a commodity. Defying the attitudes of her court, whom she accused of being 'racialist', the Queen Empress formed a close and affectionate relationship with one of them, Abdul Karim, who in 1889 was officially designated her munshi (teacher). He taught her Hindustani, and they had conversations about Indian religious and cultural life. In 1894, he was promoted – with the title of hafiz – to being her Indian secretary. But this unorthodoxy initially permitted by her status was nonetheless ultimately limited by the expectations of her role. She reported indignantly to the Prime Minister, Lord Rosebery, in 1894 that members of her Royal Household were alleging that Abdul Karim was passing confidential information to subversive contacts in India, which she refused to believe. When she went on holiday to the South of France in 1897, the Household refused to let him travel in the Queen's special train. When she was told, she swept all the papers on her desk to the floor in fury, but to no avail. There were real concerns that she was being manipulated by Abdul Karim, who in his undoubted keenness to make the most out of the Queen's favour did nothing to endear himself to other members of the royal circle. But undoubtedly class and racial prejudice were fundamental elements in his marginalization.

Meanwhile, Victoria, who was already strikingly more liberal than members of her court in her attitude towards race, was genuinely interested in finding out more about India, where she had never been, and there is some evidence that she became even more aware of the challenges posed by racial and religious difference. She developed a shrewd understanding of the interconnectedness of global politics, and the risks posed to a principled imperial rule by failure to reflect on how negative impressions were created. In 1895, in the midst of a worldwide culture war precipitated by the massacres of Armenians in the Ottoman Empire, she wrote in some distress about the inevitable side-effect of British support for the persecuted Christians – that this could be seen as opposition to Muslim culture as a whole. She expressed concern about such a zero-sum polarization, commenting that it 'was a very great danger to India to disregard the Mohammedans' feelings'.

Practising Indian politics in Britain

Dadabhai Naoroji (1825–1917) established the first Indian commercial firm in Britain in 1855. He also worked at University College, London as Professor of Gujurati from 1856 to 1865, and founded the East India Association in 1866. In 1885, he was one of the founders of the Indian National Congress. In London, he stood unsuccessfully as a parliamentary candidate for Holborn in 1886, set up the Indian Political Agency as a pressure group in Britain in 1888, and was elected as Liberal MP for Finsbury Central in 1892. His adoption as a candidate for Finsbury had been controversial, but the then prime minister Lord Salisbury's observation that a British constituency would not elect 'a black man' in fact won him some public sympathy. Having lost his seat again in 1895, in 1906 he tried again in North Lambeth, splitting the Liberal vote and coming third. In 1907, he retired to Versova, near Bombay/Mumbai. During his period in Parliament, he continued to promote causes with which he had been long associated: the opening up of the Indian Civil Service to Indians, and a demonstration of the ways in which British rule in India drained Indian financial resources. His long period in London and status both in Britain and in India made him an important figure, and his simultaneous membership of Congress and the House of Commons, whilst distinctive, signalled a generally more complicated political reality which is not always acknowledged.

Mohantas Karamchand Gandhi (1869–1948) stayed in London from 1888 to 1891, and qualified as a barrister in 1891. His period in the imperial capital enhanced his social confidence, as well as offering the opportunity to develop an understanding of Christian as well as Hindu cultures: he read the *Bible* alongside the *Bhagavad Gita*. The imaginative affinity between elements of Christian social ethics and Gandhi's political ideas was strong. Famously, Gandhi hugely admired and was inspired by the British art and social critic John Ruskin, who challenged many of the fundamental assumptions of orthodox profit-maximizing economics. Gandhi appreciated his rallying and provocative proposition that 'There is no wealth but life'.

Dramatic Devices, and Direction of the First Production

Structure

The play is in two acts, each of fifteen relatively short scenes. This structural device creates a visual and textual mosaic, which stimulates the audience in different and dynamic ways. It permits cross-cutting between different settings – Tilbury docks and Windsor Castle, for example – so as to suggest separate and parallel gendered, classed and racialized spaces, functioning simultaneously. But further conceptual connections are suggested in the imagination of the audience. The Queen and Rani can be seen in similarly contemplative mood in different physical locations at the opening of Act Two, Scene Nine. They will never meet. The principal focus of the dialogue is on Rani and Firoza, but the discussion of Hari's letters, which Rani is reading, stirs reflection in the audience both on the role of education and on the scope to use it: Rani has encouraged Hari to learn to read and write, and inspired him to read books; the Queen has been educated by Abdul Karim in Indian languages and politics. As the older ayah Firoza states categorically in Act Two, Scene Nine that the Queen has ruined India, we have a flashback to Act Two, Scene Four, in which (to the distaste of the lady-in-waiting) Abdul Karim had encouraged the Queen to follow through on her humane impulses in the face of Indian suffering. At the very end of Scene Nine, Abdul Karim comes in to see the Queen, and she simply says sorry: her power as Queen Empress is limited, and she has not even been able to prevent Abdul Karim being demoted. As an audience, we keep suggestive comparisons in our minds – in the same Scene Nine, Hari is referred to as digging in diamond mines in South Africa; Scene Ten focuses on the Diamond Jubilee of the Queen Empress in 1897. When the different worlds actually interact, first on board the ship, in the encounters of Rani and Hari with Abdul Karim, Dadabhai Naoroji and Gandhi; and then in the Ayahs' Home in London, where Dadabhai meets Rani again, we are led to speculate on the effects of intersectionality on the exercise of influence and the achievement of change.

The first production

The production of *The Empress* at the Swan Theatre in Stratford-upon-Avon in 2013 was directed by Emma Rice, who made her name with her work – as an actor and director – for Kneehigh Theatre in Cornwall. Set up in 1980, Kneehigh specialized from the beginning in site-specific productions in historic buildings and outdoor spaces, often based on myth, fairy tales or folk culture, and incorporating live music and puppets and lots of stunning visual effects. Kneehigh is now an associate company of the Bristol Old Vic and Shakespeare's Globe in London. In 2016, Rice became Artistic Director of the Globe, but parted company with them two years later, following controversy over her opening production of *A Midsummer Night's Dream* which used lighting and music to create a disco feel which was seen by the management as too populist and inauthentic. In the summer of 2018 she launched her own company, based in Bristol – Wise Children.

She embraced *The Empress* with huge enthusiasm and energy, describing it as a 'big, sprawling, epic piece'. It was her initiative to call for the music and song, seeing them as a powerful vehicle to reinforce the transcultural dynamics of the play. The production featured crossovers between classical Indian and contemporary Western idioms – with a punk rock sitar player and the opening song as a lascar rap. Colour was also used to heighten effects – as in the contrast between Rani and the Queen.

Black and white film projected onto canvas and gauze – including archival clips of the Diamond Jubilee procession and atmospheric footage of the sea – created a sense of movement and scale as a backdrop to the more miniaturized jewelled scenes taking place on platforms of different levels. Britain was symbolically presented as a tiny island in a heaving and billowing imperial sea; the royal apartments and the spaces on the ship or in London households or parks were individualized in their respective frames or suspended boxes, but in visual as well as textual dialogue with each other.

Mindful of the politics of the play, and wanting to bring out strongly its radicalism, Rice thought hard about how to avoid creating a 'costume drama', especially in light of the apparently insatiable public fascination with all things Victorian (in May 2021 a website called IHeartBritishTV.com recommended a list of '31 Great British Period Dramas Set in the Victorian Era' produced in the late twentieth and early twenty-first centuries, and currently streaming). There was a real risk of playing to stereotyped exoticism which would have compromized the impact of the play. This was avoided, and there were bold moments which worked beautifully. Perhaps the most fairy-tale magical of these occurred when Abdul Karim (in Act Two, Scene Thirteen) says that since the aged and infirm Queen cannot go to India, he will bring India to her. Flamboyantly costumed performers sing and dance, and little lit-up paper boats float over a sea of water.

The production was very positively received, although one of the ironies was that it was too expensive to transfer elsewhere, and at the time of writing the only subsequent performance has been a very small-scale one at the Royal Central School for Speech and Drama in London in 2019. Tanika Gupta commented on the distinctive impact of that production, however. Its spareness, lack of music and elaborate sets and costumes, meant that the political thrust of the text was in some ways intensified. In fact, the architecture of the play is so nicely balanced that it is possible to envisage different stagings with different sizes of cast and deployment of resources. This should be enabling for schools and colleges, where video projections, artwork and music could be created in inexpensive ways to help in the animation of a play whose text is both strong and flexible.

*   *   *

In Act One, Scene Six, Hari and Rani are at Lascar Sally's. Hari says: 'To me you are an Empress', to which Rani responds: 'I was so happy to come here. Thought I'd have such adventures and stories to tell my grandchildren. Instead I may end up begging on the streets.' In fact, as Hari predicts, she is too clever not to succeed. And he reminds her and us that her name means 'Queen'. Character and education vie with status, gender and race throughout the play, for all those in it. This drama creates adventures, and the stories emerge to tell the tale.

The Empress

Acknowledgements

The author would like to thank the following people for their insight and support in the writing of this play: Michael Boyd, Jeanie O'Hare, Pippa Hill, Rozina Visram and Emma Rice.

Characters

Rani Das, *sixteen-year-old Bengali ayah. Ages to twenty-nine years old.*

Hari Sharma, *young Indian lascar. Ages from his twenties to thirties.*

Abdul Karim, *twenty-four-year-old Indian servant to the Queen. Ages to thirty-seven years old.*

Dadabhai Naoroji, *elderly Parsi man (founder of Indian National Congress).*

Queen Victoria, *sixty-seven years of age to her death at the age of eighty-one.*

Lascar Sally, *boarding-house landlady.*

Lady Sarah, *Queen Victoria's lady-in-waiting.*

Georgina, *housekeeper to Lord John Oakham.*

Lord John Oakham, *Rani's employer.*

Firoza, *Indian ayah in her thirties.*

Serang, *captain of the lascars.*

M.K. Gandhi, *eighteen-year-old youth.*

Susan Matthews, *Rani's first employer.*

Charlotte, *English missionary.*

Mary, *English missionary.*

William, *English (Liberal) politician.*

Others: children, ayahs, lascars, Victorian English people, Indian dancers, politicians.

Ayahs = Indian nannies who looked after English children. Often in domestic servitude for life.

Lascars = sailors from the Empire used by British Empire for ships trading throughout the Indian Empire. Often termed 'the black poor'.

The Empress is set in the last fourteen years of Queen Victoria's rule, 1887–1901.

Act One: 1887

Scene One

*We are on a ship's upper deck circa 1887. We see a ragged group
of Asian sailors (lascars) busily scrubbing the deck with soap
and water. The* **Lascars** *are from all different corners of the Asian
subcontinent – Chinese, Indian and some black Africans too. All of
them are barefooted and look undernourished and dirty. They sing
as they scrub the deck.*

Song:

Lascars

> There's a Clan boat just leaving Bombay,
> Bound for old Blighty's shore;
> Heavily loaded with bum engineers,
> Bound for the land they abhor.
> She's down by the head, she's listing to port,
> She's making three knots with the tide;
> But you'll get no enjoyment from Clan Line employment,
> So come on, me lads, bless 'em all!
>
> Bless 'em all, bless 'em all;
> The Tindal, the Kasab and all;
> Bless all the 'sparkies', they're all round the twist;
> Bless all the pursers, and their limp wrists!
> If the engineers can get us home,
> The 'Kala Pani' no more will I roam;
> 'Cause you'll get no promotion, this side of the ocean,
> So cheer up, me lads, bless 'em all!

Song: 'Lascar rap'

> Head across the Arabian sea,
> Carrying opium, spices, tea.

Navigate 'round the Cape of Good Hope,
Scrub the decks or get flogged with rope.
The ports of Bombay and Calcutta,
The banks of the Ganges to London gutters.
Bless them all and serve the Empire,
Queen and country, stoke the fire.
Bombay, Mandalay, Madagascar,
Ship'd never sail without the lascars.
The ports of Canada to the Ivory Coast,
Shipping cargo to the trading posts.
So far from home, we serve the throne,
'Kala Pani' no more will I roam.
If I ever make it back to the jewel in the crown,
I'll bless them all from solid ground.*

Rani Das, *a young sixteen-year-old ayah enters. She is dressed simply in a sari and has two young English children with her. The children scamper about the deck getting in the way as the* **Lascars** *work.* **Rani** *chases after the children playing hide and seek but they evade her.*

Rani   *Ek, duy, teen, char, paach . . . Pookee*! I'm coming to get you! I can hear you! You're giggling! Where are my babies? Have they fallen in the sea?

One of the **lascars**, **Hari Sharma**, *speaks:*

Hari   Will I see you later?

Rani   I'm not sure when I can get away.

Hari   Even brats need to sleep.

Rani   Hari!

Hari   See you here?

They're here, Rani! Look!

Rani *pretends she can't see the children.*

Rani   Where? I can't see them anywhere! Where are my babies? Oh no! (*Fake fear.*) I hope they haven't fallen in the sea!

* Lyrics by Dom Coyote

Dadabhai Naoroji *enters with a young Indian man (***M.K. Gandhi** *at eighteen years old) in tow. They converse and watch the* **Lascars** *with interest. The young* **Gandhi** *looks shy and nervous whilst* **Dadabhai** *is bright, confident and sprightly.*

Lascars

> Bless 'em all, bless 'em all;
> The Tindal, the Kasab and all;
> Bless all the 'Sparkies', they're all round the twist;
> Bless all the pursers, and their limp wrists!
> If the engineers can get us home,
> The 'Kala Pani' no more will I roam;
> 'Cause you'll get no promotion, this side of the ocean,
> So cheer up, me lads, bless 'em all!

The ship's **Serang** *(Asian captain of the lascar crew) enters shouting orders and waving a thick bamboo stick (laithi) around.*

Serang   Lascar buggers. Get your backsides into it!

The captain wants to see this deck sparkly – shiny!

He waves his laithi around menacingly at the **Lascars**.

Serang *kicks* **Hari** *hard in the backside.*

Serang   You good-for-nothing lazy scoundrel, Hari. It's a wooden deck, not one of your dirty whores. You're supposed to be scrubbing, not caressing it! Anymore tomfoolery from you and I will make you climb the foremast without the ladder.

Hari *quickly scrubs harder. The* **Serang** *is directing another group of Indian and Chinese sailors as they put up banners and flags around the deck in celebration.*

Serang   Captain Ingram will be up here in ten minutes to inspect. Get this place looking like a ballroom fit for Her Majesty the Queen! You hear me?

The **Lascars** *all murmur.*

Serang   What?

Hari   Will the Queen be coming here?

Serang   How will the Queen 'be coming here', idiot, fool? Is she going to fly like a bird from the moon?

I am saying make it *fit* for the Queen or the captain sahib will be asking the cook to cut out your liver and fry it up with onions and your shrivelled little bollocks for breakfast.

Lascars (*altogether*)   Aye, aye, Serang, sir!

Serang *spits on the floor by where* **Hari** *is scrubbing.* **Hari** *daren't stop but scrubs the floor where* **Serang** *has just spat.* **Serang** *exits.*

Song:

Lascars

There is the 'Old Man', he's counting the days
'Til they will let him retire;
There stands the Chief; he's gnashing his teeth
All the coal that he's bought just won't fire.
But there's many a 'prentice just starting his time,
There's many a fool's just begun –
That's signed with 'Scots Navy' for four years of slavery,
Out here on the Hooghli run.
Bless 'em all, bless 'em all;
The Tindal, the Kasab and all;
Bless all the 'Sparkies', they're all round the twist;
Bless all the pursers, and their limp wrists!
If the engineers can get us home,
The 'Kala Pani' no more will I roam;
'Cause you'll get no promotion, this side of the ocean,
So cheer up, me lads, bless 'em all!
'Cause you'll get no promotion, this side of the ocean,
So cheer up, me lads, bless 'em all!

Rani *looks calm and savours the sun. She stands to one side and looks out to sea.*

Hari *gets up from his scrubbing and approaches* **Rani** *gingerly. He waves a small flag at her.*

Hari   For the Queen Mem Sahib. They say that she is so fat, she can't move. Always dressed in black and scowling like this.

Hari *pulls a bloated angry face.*

Rani   How do you know? You ever met her?

Hari   No. But I have seen pictures. So much money and so miserable.

Rani   What is England like Hari?

Hari   Cold.

Rani   I know about the weather. I have shawls with me.

Hari   And it rains a lot. Whole place is covered in thick, thick fog. Their buildings are big and very grand, like the ones in Calcutta. And the people are very strange.

Rani   How?

Hari   They like to look down at us from a great height.

Sometimes they can't even see us.

He holds out an apple for **Rani**.

Rani   Where did you get that from?

Hari   Last stop in Italy.

Rani *goes to take the apple but* **Hari** *holds back.*

Hari   For you, not those horrible brats of yours.

Rani   They're not horrible.

Hari   They *are* . . . baby monsters. Always squawking. They need a good *thappar* (slap).

He raises his hand and slaps imaginary children.

Rani   Stop it, Hari!

She laughs and takes the apple. She rubs it on her sari and bites into it.

Rani   Hmmm . . .

Hari *watches* **Rani** *munching happily.*

Hari   Will you marry me when we dock?

Rani   Don't be silly.

Hari   Why silly?

Rani   Because you probably have at least three wives.

Hari   I don't!

Rani   I know what you sailors are like.

She offers **Hari** *a bite of her apple.*

Hari   I am not like the others.

Rani   You are too young.

Hari   I am not! I have sailed the seas many times . . . like Sinbad. You need a man to protect you.

Rani   I can look after myself.

Hari   Of course you can.

Rani   Just watch me.

She laughs. **Hari** *watches her laugh with admiration.*

Hari   When I fall asleep, I think of you laughing.

Rani   Stop it.

Hari   Marry me.

Rani   I have a job.

She looks out to sea. **Hari** *looks at* **Rani** *wistfully.*

*An Indian man (***Abdul Karim***) takes a turn on the deck. He is proud looking, and dressed well. As he walks the* **Lascars** *move out of his way.* **Rani** *and* **Hari** *watch him approaching.*

Hari (*whispers*)   Viceroy's man. Very stuck-up.

Abdul *pauses, salaams* **Rani**.

Abdul   Abdul Karim from Agra at your service, miss.

Rani   Rani Das . . .

Abdul   Is this sailor boy bothering you?

Rani   No, I am fine . . .

Abdul (*to* **Hari**)   Get back to your work, lascar . . .

Rani   No really, thank you. There is no need to be concerned – he is my friend.

Abdul   How have you found the voyage over?

Rani   I was a little *sea sick* to begin with. It's my first time ever on a boat.

Abdul   Mine too. That storm just before we reached Aden . . . ohhh . . . I thought I was going to die.

Rani   Yes! The way the ship swayed from side to side. The children in my charge suffered terribly. Poor little things.

Abdul   You must serve them well, Rani.

Rani   They are my darlings.

Abdul *takes out a silver compass and looks at it and then out to sea.*

Rani *looks at it intrigued.*

Rani   Oh! That's beautiful . . . what is it?

Abdul   A compass.

Rani   I've never see one of those before.

Abdul   It belonged to my father. Look, you place it flat on your hand and the magnet inside it connects to the earth's magnetic force. North, south, east, west.

Rani   The hands are swinging 'round . . . is that north?

Abdul   Yes, which is the direction of our destination.

Rani   How clever!

Abdul   May Allah keep you safe and shine his blessings upon you.

Rani   And upon you too.

Abdul   *Shukria.*

Hari *does not like the look of* **Abdul**.

Abdul   A word of advice, Miss Das – you should choose your friends more carefully in future.

Abdul *gives* **Hari** *a dirty look and then moves on.*

Hari   Bloody cheek. Might be all dressed up like a fancy peacock but he is still a lackee to the white man.

The **Serang** *reappears behind* **Hari**, *grabs and twists his ear and leads him away from* **Rani**. **Hari** *cries out in pain.*

Hari   Aaagghhh . . . aaahhh . . .

Serang   And you are lackee to this black man. Lazy arse . . . get back to work or I will send your skinny little body down to hell to work in the boiler room.

The **Serang** *gives* **Hari** *another good kick and* **Hari** *scurries back to his bucket.*

Dadabhai *is speaking loudly to* **Gandhi**. **Rani** *can't help but eavesdrop.*

Dadabhai   What is scandalous, undemocratic and therefore un-British is that the Indian population pay the taxes but have no voice in the government of India.

Gandhi   This is the work you have been undertaking for the East India Association?

Dadabhai   And cataloguing the gradual impoverishment of our country. All our resources are steadily drained out through European pay-packets.

Gandhi   When you put it like that, Dadabhai . . .

So we need reform the system. And to get some representatives in the Imperial Parliament.

Dadabhai   Precisely. But in that respect, I have failed to gain a seat. According to Lord Salisbury it is because an English constituency is not ready to elect a 'black man', to represent them.

Gandhi (*shocked*)   He called you a black man?

Dadabhai   He did.

He turns and sees **Rani**.

Dadabhai   Ahhh . . . Rani . . . How are you this fine morning?

Rani   Excited to be finally nearing land.

She does namaste. **Gandhi** *shyly returns the namaste.*

Dadabhai   We have been watching with interest the work of our fellow Indian sailors. Tell Rani what you have to say on the subject, Gandhi?

Gandhi *is too shy to speak.*

Dadabhai   Speak up, my dear fellow. You must have more confidence in your opinions.

Gandhi   From what one can see, the lascars are treated with utter inhumanity by the head serang.

Dadabhai   And yet, without all their efforts, we would have been lost at sea.

They all turn and watch the **Lascars** *at work.*

Rani   They work so hard . . .

Dadabhai   Have you noticed that the English sailors seem to have an easier time of it?

Gandhi   It is most unjust.

Dadabhai   Spoken like a true lawyer, Gandhi.

Gandhi   A lawyer in waiting, Dadabhai.

Dadabhai   Study hard, young man. And for goodness' sake, you must speak up. How are you going to represent anyone with that quiet voice of yours?

Rani   Is that what you are going to do in England, Mr Gandhi? Become a lawyer?

Gandhi   That is the plan. But also I wish to be an English gentleman – learn to dance, to play the violin, to speak French and to improve my English.

Dadabhai   With all those skills you'll be quite the socialite – Gandhi the dandy!

Gandhi   Oh no, I made an oath to my mother not to partake of meat, wine or women.

Rani   I will be standing in the same city as the Queen of England. Somewhere, she will be close by, breathing the same air. Imagine that?! Can I visit her?

Dadabhai   I don't think so. The Queen is rather hidden away from everyday people.

Gandhi   I trust you will be taken care of in England?

Rani   I am in service to a very kind lady and gentleman. I will be looking after their children.

Dadabhai   Bless you, my child. I pray you are treated well by your employers and that you will get a chance to educate yourself as you wish. Education is the only path to freedom.

The **Serang** *drives the* **Lascars** *to work harder. We end the scene with the lascar song from the beginning of the play.*

Song:

Lascars

> If the seas can get us home,
> 'Kala Pani' no more will I roam;
> 'Cause you'll get no promotion, this side of the ocean
> So cheer up, me lads, bless 'em all!

Scene Two

It is night time. We are on the moonlit deck of the boat and **Rani** *is sat with* **Hari** *reading by the light of a hurricane lamp. The stars are out and the sea is calm.*

Rani (*reads*)

> Water, water, everywhere,
> And all the boards did shrink;
> Water, water, everywhere,
> Nor any drop to drink.

Hari (*reads falteringly*)

> I closed my lids, and kept them close,
> And the balls like pulses beat;
> For the sky and the sea, and the sea and the sky
> Lay like a load on my weary eye,
> And the dead were at my feet.

Rani   You are reading very well.

Hari *puts down the book.*

Hari   He shouldn't have killed the albatross.

Rani   Do you like the poem?

Hari   We navigate by the stars and the winds but I understand this poem. It is terrible to be lost on the sea in a mist.

He gets up and paces.

Rani   Have you ever thought of making your living in England?

Hari   I tried it once. Became an apprentice with a carpenter. Used to be good at carving wood. Made chairs with my grandfather back home. But no, it didn't work out.

Rani   If you learnt your letters, you could get a job as a clerk.

Hari *laughs long and hard.*

Rani   Why are you laughing?

Hari   Because I am stupid with letters.

Rani   You're not! Look how much you've achieved in these few weeks! You're a quick learner, Hari.

Hari   My grandfather started to teach me, but then he died and that was the end of my lessons.

Rani   It's never too late and I can teach you.

Hari *looks at* **Rani***, grateful.*

Hari   You have a kind heart.

Rani   If you come to where I work every day, even for half an hour, we can sit outside and read together.

Hari   I'm a sailor, Rani. How would I earn money to eat?

Rani   You can find work somewhere . . . it's a big city. There must be work.

Hari   You want me to stay near you?

Rani *looks coy.*

Hari   You like me that much?

Rani   When I have finished with you, you will be able to read the newspapers.

Hari *reaches over and holds her hand.*

Hari   Then you will have to be my teacher for a long time.

They hear the sound of a fiddle playing on the deck.

Hari   I wish I was a wealthy man. Then we could be married and you wouldn't need to work as a servant for English families.

Rani   Who said I want to marry you? And I like working!

Hari   I love you, Rani.

Rani   Don't be silly.

Hari   Don't laugh at me. I know I have nothing to offer you. But I could make you very happy.

Hari *edges closer to* **Rani***, placing his arm around her.*

Rani (*laughs*)   Stop it. Hari.

Hari   The first time I saw you on this boat, I felt I had known you in another life . . . that we had been together . . . seeing you made me feel like a sailor feels when he has been drifting on an endless swell of sea and then he spots the land. The relief! The joy! Knowing that he will stand on firm ground.

Rani *and* **Hari** *get closer. They kiss.*

Susan Matthews   RANI! RANI! Please see to the children!

They have woken up!

Rani *pulls back. She smooths down her hair and sari.*

Rani (*calls back*)   Yes, Mrs Matthews. Coming!

(*To* **Hari**.) I have to go.

Rani *smiles and exits.* **Hari** *stands on the deck wistfully.* **Rani** *returns for one last kiss and then disappears inside again.*

Scene Three

Windsor Castle, 1887.

It is early morning. **Queen Victoria** *(in her late sixties) is sat on a chair, her breakfast things laid before her. She is eating an egg from a golden egg cup. Her lady-in-waiting* **Lady Sarah** *is by her side.*

Victoria   Such crowds yesterday. Such enormous good humour. All the balconies were crammed with people cheering with flags.

Lady Sarah   They all love their Queen and Sovereign.

Victoria   The decorations along Piccadilly were quite beautiful and so many touching inscriptions. Such waving of hands.

Lady Sarah   It has been an exhausting couple of days for you.

Victoria   We must write it all down before we forget the details.

Lady Sarah   Of course, ma'am.

Victoria   It's a shame those children sang 'God Save the Queen' so out of tune . . .

She giggles.

Lady Sarah   Appallingly out of tune actually . . . Bless them.

Victoria   To think, this day fifty years ago we went to St James's Palace for our proclamation . . . Fifty years ago . . . our robes beautifully draped on the chair.

Lady Sarah   You looked glorious, ma'am, both then and today.

Victoria   How do you know how we looked back then, Lady Sarah? You were just a child.

Lady Sarah   I have seen the portraits.

Victoria   Indeed. How we sat there yesterday without our darling Albert by our side . . . he would have been so proud of me.

Lady Sarah *looks sympathetically across at* **Victoria**.

Offstage **Abdul** *coughs.*

Lady Sarah   Ma'am, I wondered if this would be a good time to inform you of . . . erm . . .

Victoria   My dear Lady Sarah, what is it?

Lady Sarah   Sir John Tyler has a special gift he wanted to present to you.

Victoria   Sir John . . .?

Lady Sarah   Ma'am, he's the governor of the north-west provinces in India and he is sending you a rather unusual golden anniversary presentation.

Victoria   Well, let us see.

Lady Sarah *peruses the contents of a letter.*

Lady Sarah   He writes to you here that the presentation is on its way on a boat and should reach you within the week.

Victoria   What is this 'unusual presentation'?

Lady Sarah   He does not say. Simply writes here that 'I have sent my Queen and Sovereign a surprise'.

Victoria *looks put out.*

Victoria   We do not care for surprises.

Lady Sarah *looks concerned.*

Scene Four

*We are now at Tilbury docks. Passengers have disembarked from
the ship and are looking around for their friends and families.
Everyone looks relieved to be on land.*

Rani *is counting the luggage as it is brought out by* **Lascars**. *She
is also trying to manage the children who are running around her
excitedly.*

Child One   Land ahoy! Land ahoy! We're home!

Rani   George . . . George . . . please . . . behave yourself. Your
father will be cross . . . look at your shirt . . . George!

Lascar   I think that is all, memsahib.

Rani   No. There was a large trunk too.

The **Lascar** *scratches his head.*

Rani   Go and have a look. It was in the same section with all the
other cases.

The **Lascar** *heads off to look for the trunk.* **Hari** *rushes forward to
speak with* **Rani**. *Suddenly he looks awkward as he sees* **Dadabhai**
and **Gandhi** *walking up to* **Rani**. *(*Hari *is very aware of his low
status here and hovers.)*

Gandhi *looks nervously about him.*

Dadabhai   This is where we say our farewells, young woman.

Rani   Mr Gandhi, good luck with the law and the French lessons.

Gandhi   Thank you. And may God watch over you.

Oh look! I can see my uncle has come to meet me.

Dadabhai   I will join you in a moment, Gandhi.

Gandhi *does a very polite namaste and exits hurriedly.*

Dadabhai   So, Rani! Your big adventure begins.

Rani   Thank you, Dadabhai.

Daabhai   For what?

Rani   For looking out for me on the voyage.

Dadabhai   My child, you have an enquiring mind.

Don't let it go to waste please. Read, read and read some more.

He places his hand on **Rani***'s head in blessing and exits hurriedly.*

Susan Matthews *approaches.*

Susan   What a relief to have the ground beneath my feet again.

Hari *backs away.*

Susan   Rani – is that all our luggage?

Rani   Just one more to come.

Susan   Thank you.

Rani   The children are so excited to be on firm ground again.
It is hard to get used to . . . keep expecting the earth to sway like
this . . .

She sways as if she is on a ship. She laughs happily.

Susan *looks bored.*

Rani   I'm sorry, madam, I feel slightly light-headed . . . so long at
sea . . .

Susan   Believe me, we all feel the same way. It was a very
tiresome journey.

*She reaches into her skirt pocket and pulls out an envelope. She
tries to hand it to* **Rani** *who looks bemused.*

Susan   Payment for your work, Rani, plus a little bonus.

You have been most helpful in the voyage across.

Rani *timidly takes the envelope and bows her thanks.*

Rani   Has the carriage been ordered, madam?

Shall I . . .?

Susan   My man is on his way – yes. But we . . . that is Mr Matthews and myself have no further need of your services now.

Rani *looks up at* **Susan** *– perplexed.*

Rani   I am sorry, madam, I don't understand.

Susan (*to* **Rani**)   There's money in there for a month, for lodgings, and a letter of reference.

Rani   Lodgings?

Susan   You're a clever girl. You'll find your way around.

Rani *gathers the children around her who cling to her. The* **Lascar** *approaches carrying a large and heavy trunk.*

Lascar   Found it, memsahib! It was hiding in the back, under lots of ropes . . . had to really hunt around for it . . .

Hari *realises what is happening and hushes the other* **Lascar** *up.* **Susan** *hurriedly tips the* **Lascar***.*

Susan   Take our bags to the carriage over there please.

The **Lascar** *does her bidding.*

Rani   But, madam, you said I would have a position here. That is why I came. To look after the children.

Child One   We like Rani! We want her to stay with us!

Susan   I'm afraid that's quite out of the question.

We already have a nanny, an English one.

Rani   But you said . . .

Susan   I changed my mind. We have no need for you. The children need a governess, someone to help them with their education.

Rani   But I can do everything else. I can sew and clean and cook.

Susan   Rani. We really have no further use for you.

The children start to cry and cling to **Rani**. **Susan** *looks irritated.*

Susan   Don't be silly, children, now come with me and your father.

She tries to pull her children, but they refuse to move and cry louder. **Rani** *is crying too.*

Rani   But where will I go? Where will I find work?

I am a complete stranger in this country.

Susan   That is not my problem.

Rani   You are breaking your word to me. My mother looked after you, memsahib.

Susan   Your mother was different. She was a seasoned and experienced ayah. You are not.

Rani   But I can learn and there was an agreement.

Susan   No written contract you understand.

Rani   Doesn't a verbal agreement between families mean something . . .?

Susan   It is not legally binding.

Rani   Then why did you bring me? Why did you lie to my mother and promise her you would look after me?

Susan   How dare you call me a liar!

Rani   You have broken your word to my mother.

Hari (*calls out*)   Please . . . Mrs Matthews . . . Memsahib . . . please, you can't just abandon her here! You can't! She is only a young girl. She knows nothing of the ways of the world.

Susan   I do not talk to vagabond sailors.

Look at it this way, Rani, we're giving you your freedom.

Rani *rushes forwards and grabs the hem of* **Susan**'s *dress.* **Rani** *falls on her knees.* **Abdul** *disembarks the boat and watches the scene unfold.*

Rani   Memsahib, please. I will be lost . . . there is no hope for me . . .

Susan   You will tear my dress. Unhand me at once.

Passers-by stare at the two women. **Susan** *is embarrassed.*

Rani (*angry now*)   I looked after your children, I bathed them, fed them, sang them songs to get them to sleep . . . just as my mother did for you!

Susan   And you were both in turn – paid and fed.

Rani   You have known me since I was a child.

Have you no feeling for me?

Susan   You are a grown woman now, Rani. If you do not like it here, you can catch the next ship back. There is enough money there for your passage.

As for feeling . . . you are merely my servant's offspring. Now take your filthy hands off my dress.

Rani *flinches as though she has been dealt a blow. She lets go of* **Susan**'s *dress.*

The little girl looks up at **Rani**.

Child Two   I love you, Rani.

Then she tears herself away from **Rani** *and obediently walks away with her mother.* **Susan** *exits without a backward glance.* **Rani** *is distraught.* **Hari** *watches her grief and feels terrible for her.*

Abdul *helps* **Rani** *up. He sits her down and* **Hari** *fetches her some water.*

Rani   I don't know anyone here. What kind of people are they?

Hari *stands close by and watches.*

Abdul   You must be brave, little Rani.

I would take you with me but I am under strict instructions. You must find employment. In a good house.

Rani   I don't know how to.

Abdul   Look, they have given you references, use them to find work.

Rani   I cannot believe that they could be so cruel.

Abdul   The ways of the world can be cruel, my little friend. That is why you must think of yourself first. Always. Take care of your own interests.

He looks around him, helplessly.

I have to go, I am being summoned.

He gives **Rani** *a gift.*

Abdul   Take my compass as a good luck charm.

Rani   I can't take this. It's yours!

Abdul   I don't need it. I know where I'm going.

Use it well and it will always lead you to the right place.

He salaams **Rani** *and exits. As he exits he looks back at* **Rani**, *sad to leave her in so much distress.* **Rani** *sits and sobs.* **Hari** *approaches.*

Hari   I'm sorry, I've seen it too many times before.

Young men and women . . . we come like idiots hoping for a better life.

Rani   I thought I had a position.

Hari   You'll get another one.

Rani   I was going to send money home. To my mother . . . for my little brother's schooling . . . I thought, a couple of years here and then I will go back with the Matthews and . . .

Hari   Maybe it is all for the best.

Rani   How? My family are depending on me.

Hari *looks at* **Rani** *with a mixture of pity and love. He takes her bundle off her.*

Hari   No point wailing. First we have to get a roof over your head, then we deal with the other problem. Come. Come with me, Rani. I will find you a place to stay. It is too cold to sleep outside and soon it will be dark. At least this 'vagabond sailor' knows his way around this city.

Rani *sits and cries.*

Hari   Rani. I will look after you. Please don't flood London with your tears.

He extends his hand. **Rani** *hesitates before taking it and getting up slowly to follow him.*

Scene Four B

Queen Victoria *is sat on her own reading letters.* **Lady Sarah** *enters and curtseys to* **Victoria***.*

Lady Sarah   Ma'am, Sir John Tyler's presentation has arrived.

Victoria   Ah. Our surprise. Let us see.

Lady Sarah *turns to call* **Abdul** *in.* **Abdul** *enters.* **Victoria** *looks astonished.*

Lady Sarah   This is . . . erm . . . (**Lady Sarah** *peruses a letter.*)
Erm . . .

Abdul *steps forward and bows with a flourish.*

Abdul   Abdul Karim.

Victoria *sits forward in her chair.*

Lady Sarah (*reads a letter*)   'Her Majesty, etc, etc . . .
to mark her fiftieth anniversary on the British throne, Sir John

Tyler presents Her Majesty with a most excellent Indian servant from the city of Agra. He can cook Indian curry and has a most excellent temperament.'

She stares at **Abdul**.

Lady Sarah   I suppose I could give this man a small tour of the royal grounds, put him up in the servants' quarters for a few weeks' vacation and then send him back, with our deepest apologies and gracious thanks of course.

Victoria   Send him back?

Lady Sarah   He cannot stay here. He probably doesn't even speak English. How will we communicate with him?

Victoria   Do you speak English?

Abdul *smiles coquettishly.*

Abdul   English is one of several languages I am fluent in, Your Royal Highness.

Victoria   And have you always lived in Agra?

Abdul   I was born there, ma'am, as indeed my father and his father before him were. My father is a surgeon in the Indian army.

Lady Sarah   An actual medical physician?

Abdul   Yes, Your Ladyship.

Lady Sarah *doesn't like the flirtatious nature of* **Abdul**.

Lady Sarah   Ma'am, shall I arrange for his transportation back to India?

Victoria *eyes* **Abdul** *for a while.*

Victoria   Indeed not. We have already decided.

He will attend us, behind our chair every morning as we take breakfast.

We are after all the Empress of India and it is only fitting that we should be waited upon by such a noble gentleman of that land. Besides, look! His turban matches our egg cup.

Victoria *and* **Abdul** *share the joke and smile at each other.* **Lady Sarah** *does not laugh.*

Victoria   Mr Karim. What do you have in that box there?

Abdul *steps forward offering the box.* **Lady Sarah** *is jumpy.*

Abdul   It is a gift for you from my country.

Lady Sarah   Please, Your Majesty, do not open it until I have perused the contents.

Victoria *is very excited. She takes the box and runs her hands over the gem stones.* **Lady Sarah** *stands close by and stares at the box, afraid.*

Victoria   Such exquisite workmanship.

Abdul   Precious rubies and pearls, Your Majesty.

All inlaid in gold to celebrate your glorious Golden Jubilee.

Victoria   How thoughtful, how beautiful. Please accept our heartfelt thanks. We think there is something inside?

Abdul *looks at* **Victoria** *in the eyes.*

Abdul   Your Majesty need only slip the catch to open it and see.

Lady Sarah   Your Majesty, I must insist!

Victoria *does not listen but opens the box.*

Victoria   The aroma . . . it is very . . . strong . . . but sweet . . .

Lady Sarah *peers in the box too, unable to hide her curiosity.*

Lady Sarah   What is this?

Abdul   Indian spices, Your Majesty, so I may cook curries for you. It is a spice box.

Victora   How wonderful!

Lady Sarah   Curry will not do at all for the royal digestion.

Victoria   We like curry.

Lady Sarah   It is not practical, ma'am. The Master of the House will be greatly displeased to have to find work for this Indian. And what will the royal chef say?

Victoria *looks at* **Lady Sarah** *with displeasure.*

Lady Sarah   Ma'am?

Victoria   We do not care for the Master of the House and his petty prejudices. He will have to do as we say. And the chef will have to make way for Mr Karim.

Lady Sarah   But ma'am, we have never before had male Indian servants in the royal household. Surely, this needs some discussion with Prince Edward? There are issues of security and decency.

Victoria   We have decided.

She holds up her hand to stay **Lady Sarah** *who realises she has lost the battle. She motions to* **Abdul** *who walks around to stand in attendance behind* **Victoria**.

Lady Sarah   You may only speak to Her Majesty when you are spoken to, you may not look directly at Her Majesty, you will bow after each sentence communicated with her and, as far as possible, you will not turn your back on Her Majesty when leaving the room. You will not engage in idle chatter at any time whilst in her presence. You will address her as . . .

Victoria *taps her egg cup.*

Victoria (*interrupting*)   It has always been a source of major disappointment to us that we have not been able to make the journey to our Indian Empire. At last we have an Indian gentleman who will be able to enlighten us on the habits and customs of our subjects so far away.

I *want* him to talk to me.

She turns and looks at **Abdul** *who stares straight ahead. She looks delighted.* **Lady Sarah** *looks worried.*

Scene Five

We are in **Lascar Sally***'s boarding house. It is a rowdy place. We can see many* **Lascars** *– Chinese, Indian, Indonesian, from all parts of the world. Some are drinking and eating at tables. Others are playing cards whilst others are singing traditional songs from their country. There are a couple of women there too – white English as well as black who are very obviously prostitutes and are touting their wares to the men. The scene is of debauchery and poverty.*

Song: 'Shanty rap'

Lascars

> Rats and beggars and drunks and whores,
> Drinking in the gutters 'til the break of dawn.
> These streets aren't paved with gold,
> Just pigeon shit and pea-green mould.
> Always raining and it's damn bloody cold,
> So stoke up the fire and shovel in the coal.
> In London town by the banks of the Thames,
> There's the flute and the fiddle of the dirty old men.
> When the snow calls and the cold wind blows,
> I'll be dreaming of me Chori and the shores of home.
> So I'll take my chances on Tilbury docks,
> Last one on board is bound to get flogged.*

Lascar Sally, *the owner, is cussing a sailor in fluent Hindi.*

Sally (*in Hindi*)   *Mené tum ko bola, aapne besurat shakal. yahan sé lejan har sa mé hangama or tamasha. Dafa ho jao. Haramzada! Sala! Kamina!*

(I told you, I don't want to see your ugly face in here again. Always fighting, always causing a commotion. Now get your sorry arse out of here! Bastard! Time waster!)

AND DON'T COME BACK!

* Lyrics by Dom Coyote

The sailor shouts abuse back in Hindi before stumbling out.

Hari *leads* **Rani** *in just as* **Sally** *is bundling a sailor out.*

Rani *looks around her in horror.*

Hari   This is where I stay when I am on land in England.

Rani *looks around her speechless.*

Hari   We can get a room for the night here.

Some **Lascars** *come forward to greet* **Hari***. They pull him in, delighted to see him. There is much camaraderie and back slapping, a lot of cheering.* **Rani** *slips off to one side and sits quietly out of sight.*

Sally   Hari! Good to see you!

Lascar One   Hari! Look at you! Skinnier than ever.

Hari   Sameer, drunker than ever. Is that Mohammed?

Lascar Three *has his head in a bandage.*

Lascar Three   No, it is Mohammed's uncle. Who d'you think it is?

Hari   Last time I saw you . . .

Lascar Three   A year and a half ago, down in Madras.

That bloody ship full of Chinamen and illegal opium. Remember?

Hari   What happened to your head?

Sally   The ship's captain decided to use it as a punch bag.

Lascar Three   Accused me of stealing his pocket watch!

Me?

Can you believe that?

Lascar One *pulls out a gold pocket watch from* **Lascar Three***'s pocket.*

Hari   Mohammed!

Lascar Three   He refused to pay me. I took my own wages.

Lascar Two   I heard your ship had docked. How was the voyage?

Hari   This time, not so bad. Serang Ali was a devil though. My backside is sore from the kickings he gave me.

Sally   As long as it was just kickings he gave your arse and nothing more . . .

Everyone laughs. **Hari** *looks embarrassed for* **Rani***'s sake.*

Lascar Three   He thinks he is the King of the Seas.

Lascar One   On that ship he is.

Lascar Two   You mean that bucket? It has more holes in it than your brain.

Hari   How long are you all here for?

Lascar One   Tomorrow I set sail for the West Indies.

Lascar Two   And next week we sail for the Cape.

Lascar One   Hey, Hari, you hear that the *Brittania* was wrecked off the coast of Madagascar?

Hari   No?

Lascar One   Almost all the lascar crew drowned. Not enough lifeboats and they were so weak, they could hardly swim, even though the shore was near.

Hari   How many?

Lascar Two   Officially twenty-five, unofficially one hundred and twenty-five.

Hari   But wait! Akbar was on that ship wasn't he?

Lascar Three   Yes . . .

Hari   Any word from him?

All the **Lascars** *look around at each other and shake their heads.*

Hari   Maybe he survived. He was a strong swimmer, a good sailor . . . he will have swum to shore – No?

Lascar Two   They were a weak and starving crew. There was dysentery and cholera on board. No food and what little there was went to the English officers.

Hari *looks upset.*

Hari   I hope Akbar made it – we had some good times together . . . Have you seen him, Sally? Has Akbar been here?

Sally   Sorry, love – no. Actually Hari *you* look like you need a good meal.

Hari   Starving.

Lascar Three   And a stiff drink. Sally has concocted some special fire water for us today. Heats you up.

Sally   I brewed it extra strong – just how you like it, Hari.

Hari   No drinking.

Lascar One   Why not?

Hari   I have a guest I must look after.

Lascar Three   Guest?

All the **Lascars** *turn at once and see* **Rani** *as if for the first time.*

Lascar Two   Hari! Who is this pretty flower of a guest you have brought with you?

Lascar Three   A princess.

Lascar Two   A dancer?

Lascar One   Does she like two at a time?

Hari *rushes to* **Rani**'s *side.*

Hari   Oi!

Gradually everyone crowds around **Rani** *who tries to make herself as small as possible. A couple of the women come forward and touch her hair and her dress, and someone tries to pull her bundle of clothes away from her.* **Sally** *shoos everyone off.*

Sally (*in Hindi*)   *Béchari ko saas lené do hato, hato!* (Stop crowding 'round the poor girl . . . c'mon, give her some air . . . move, move!)

Who is this poor creature, Hari? Why you brought her here?

Hari   She is my friend . . . Rani . . . her employers abandoned her at the docks.

Lascar One   Ayah?

Hari   Yes.

Sally   Poor darlin', she's just a child. She looks terrified.

Rani   I'm sixteen.

Lascar One (*nudges* **Hari**)   Old enough then, eh?

Everyone laughs.

Sally   Are you in love again Hari?

Lascar Two   She's prettier than the last one.

Hari   Please . . .

Sally (*to* **Rani**)   Did he offer to marry you too?

Lascar One   He makes marriage proposals to everyone.

Hari *squirms.* **Rani** *looks upset.*

Hari   Don't listen to them.

Sally   Word of warning, petal – they all beg for your hand and then they leave you when they've got what they wanted.

Hari (*to* **Rani**)   They are just pulling your leg.

Sally   Sailors, eh?! I've had enough of them as husbands, so I should know.

Lascar Two   Four husbands.

Lascar Four   Four husbands – the other hundred were just men.

Sally   Shut up! Have some respect. If it wasn't for me, you'd have to sleep in the streets. No one else will put you lot up.

Lascar Three   Sorry, Sally. You know we respect and adore you.

Lascar Two   Adore you.

Hari   Sally, please look after Rani for me . . . she is lost.

Sally   I can see that for myself. This your first night in England?

Rani *nods.*

Sally   Poor love's trembling like a leaf. Don't be frightened child. No harm will come to you here. My name is Sally. I will look after you. Come, we'll get some nice warm broth inside you.

The **Women** *both pull* **Rani** *to one side; they shoo the* **Lascar** *aside.*

Sally (*in Hindi*)   *Kya dekh rahé ho*?

(Stop gawping will ya?)

Can't you see the girl's frightened?

Sally *leads* **Rani** *away to the side.* **Rani** *goes with them warily.* **Hari** *cranes his neck, anxious about* **Rani***, but then gets pulled away by his fellow* **Lascars***. He resists and keeps trying to go back to* **Rani** *but his friends are persistent and they ply him with drink. They sing a bawdy song.*

Lascars (*sing*)

There's nothing for dinner, there's nothing for tea,
And that second steward keeps winking at me.
He and the cook are a bloody disgrace;
Just see the look on the galley boy's face!

The mate is a bastard, the second's a drunk
The third reads dirty books in his bunk;
As for the old man, no one can say;
No bugger's seen him since we sailed away.

Scene Six

We are in a tiny room/hovel with a threadbare mattress on the floor. The sounds of the **Lascars**' *revelry can be heard from below.* **Hari** *is lying drunk on the mattress singing a song.* **Rani** *is crouched in the corner looking scared and miserable.*

Hari (*humming*)

> There's nothing for dinner, there's nothing for tea,
> And that second steward keeps winking at me.
> He and the cook are a bloody disgrace;
> Just see the look on the galley boy's face!

How are you?

Rani *does not speak.*

Hari   Hai, hai, Rani. Come on . . . cheer up. You're in London now . . .

Hari *slaps the space on the mattress next to him.*

Rani *smarts and turns her face to the wall. She cries.* **Hari** *sits up on his elbow and tries to focus on her.*

Rani   It smells in here . . .

Hari   That's just the damp . . . old building . . .

Rani   And you're drunk.

Hari   Yes . . . yes . . . I think I am.

He starts to giggle.

Rani   This place . . . bad people . . . bad women . . . I am not that kind of woman.

Hari   No one says you are a bad woman, Rani.

Come, lie down, get some sleep . . . I am tired too.

Rani   How could you bring me to this place . . . how could you think . . .? I want to go home.

Hari   We all want to go home. But what is there?

Poverty, people dying of starvation, no jobs, nothing.

Rani   I hate it here.

Hari   Tomorrow . . . we can go to the docks . . . see if you can get passage . . .

Rani   Have there been many other women, Hari?

Hari   What?

Rani   Am I just one of many stupid young girls you bring back here?

Hari   Stop talking rubbish.

Rani *stands and screams.*

Hari   What? What? Shhhh . . .

Rani *stares in horror at a spot in the room.*

Rani   I saw a rat . . . there . . . there!

Hari *laughs.*

Hari   Is that all? This is London – it is full of rats.

Rani *rushes over to* **Hari** *who holds her.*

Hari   You are a big baby, Rani Das. And I love you.

He giggles again. He falls back on the bed.

Come and lie down. We are friends, yes?

He cuddles **Rani** *and sings her a folky song from Bengal to make her feel at ease.* **Rani** *joins in falteringly.* **Hari** *strokes her face.*

Hari   There, that's better isn't it? I am sorry, Rani.

To be honest, Lascar Sally's is the only place that would take us for the night, so I had no choice. There are many people from our land who end up living on the streets, starving, begging.

Rani   In my village, guests are treated as gods.

Hari   That is the problem. We were too nice to the foreigners and so they decided to stay and then started bossing us around our own home.

Rani   After all these years, my mistress only saw me as 'the offspring of her servant'.

She and **Hari** *embrace.*

Hari   To me, you are an empress.

Rani   I was so happy to come here. Thought I'd have such adventures and stories to tell my grandchildren. Instead I may end up begging on the streets.

Hari   Rani – your name means 'queen'. You could never become a beggar – you're too clever.

One day, I will make my fortune. There are diamond mines in Africa. I just need to find one little shiny piece of glass and then you and I could live happily. Go back home, buy you expensive silk saris and me, I don't want much – just a pair of nice shoes. You could open a school.

Rani   Yes! I would love that!

Hari   You are a natural born teacher.

And I could make all the furniture in our house. Tables, a little rocking chair, a rocking horse even!

Rani   Rocking horse?

Hari   For our children to play on. A girl called Lata, after my mother.

Rani   And a boy called Prasad after my grandfather.

They both laugh excitedly. **Hari** *kisses* **Rani**. *She kisses back.*

Hari   I will be your man and you will be my woman. We will watch our children grow and we will grow old together.

They kiss again but when **Hari** *tries to take it further,* **Rani** *pushes him off.*

Hari   What? We were getting on well.

Rani   No. Not like this. Not in this place.

Hari   Rani . . .

Rani   No, Hari. It is not what I want.

Rani *gets up and crouches in the corner of the room again.*

Hari   Suit yourself. I thought you liked me.

He turns his back on **Rani** *and falls asleep.* **Rani** *sits and stares at him.*

Song: 'Cast adrift the starlight'

Reeling in the night,
Twilight turning the tide,
A city with a cautious sun.
Sky full of amber, calling
The daylight falling
In circles on the shoreline.

Cast adrift the starlight,
Souls all sailing out in the dark.
Cast adrift the starlight,
Follow the compass of a wheeling heart.

Watching the sparks,
Beacons burning apart
The dream of a distant sun.
Ocean full of amber, calling
'Til midnight falls
In circles on the shoreline.
Cast adrift the starlight,
Souls all sailing out in the dark.
Cast adrift the starlight,
Follow the compass of a wheeling heart.*

As night descends and the revelry downstairs quietens down, **Rani** *takes out the compass* **Abdul** *gave her and places it in the palm of her hand. She stares at it for some time and then gets up and leaves the room.*

* Lyrics by Dom Coyote

In the morning light, **Hari** *sits up in bed and holds his aching head. He looks around the room.*

Hari   Rani?

He gets up and calls out.

Rani! (*Shouts louder*.) Rani! Rani!

Sally *enters, dishevelled hair.*

Sally   Stop your hollering, Hari. Everyone's sleeping.

Hari   Is she downstairs?

Sally   She's just gone.

Hari   Gone? Where?

Sally   I dunno. She left you a note though.

She fands over a note to **Hari**.

Hari   She'll get lost . . . she doesn't know her way around . . . how will she . . .?

He stares confused at the piece of paper. (He can't read very well.)

Sally   Read it then . . . what's it say?

Hari   I can't focus . . . the drink last night. Oohhh . . . my head. Can you read it?

Sally   How can I? It's all in Bengali. I dunno what you did to her last night . . . heard her screaming.

Hari   Screaming?

Sally   Nearly sent the cavalry in but . . .

Hari   She was afraid of a rat.

Sally   Got a lot of scary times ahead of her then, hasn't she?

Hari   She didn't say where she was going?

Sally   No. Basically her ladyship was too good for this place and she's scarpered.

You tried to take advantage of her didn't you?

Hari *looks ashamed.*

Sally   You men, you're all the same.

Hari   She doesn't know anything about this city.

Sally   She'll learn soon enough to fend for herself.

Just pray that she don't end up in the workhouse . . . or worse. She's a pretty girl and we all know what happens to pretty girls in this city. Alright, show's over.

She exits. **Hari** *looks at the letter, upset.*

Scene Seven

Windsor Castle.

Victoria *is sitting at breakfast.* **Abdul** *is serving* **Victoria** *some food.* **Lady Sarah** *is sitting nearby doing some embroidery and watching like a hawk.*

Victoria   Thank you, Abdul.

Abdul *bows.*

Victoria   How are you today?

Abdul   Thank you for asking, Your Majesty. Sadly, I am not, shall we say, in the peak of health.

Victoria   Nothing serious we hope?

Abdul   I have caught a slight chill, ma'am. I am just unused to the climate . . . it will take some time.

Victoria   Lady Sarah, perhaps we should ask Dr Reid to take a look at Mr Karim?

Lady Sarah   I shall arrange it, though I suspect the doctor has more pressing engagements seeing to the royal members of the house.

Abdul *coughs ostentatiously.*

Abdul   Lady Sarah is right. I suspect it is simply a cold that will pass.

Victoria   And are your sleeping quarters to your liking?

Abdul   They are sufficient to my requirement, ma'am, thank you.

Lady Sarah   I would have thought that the royal servants' quarters would have been more than 'sufficient'.

Abdul *smiles and bows.*

Abdul   Just a little drafty.

Lady Sarah *is amazed at* **Abdul**'s *nerve.*

Lady Sarah   I understand Indian blood is thinner than the English. You must feel the cold more than we do.

Victoria   Is that a biological fact, Lady Sarah? Surely we all have the same corpuscles and blood cells. We share all the same human physiology, do we not?

Lady Sarah   Yes, but there are differences, Your Majesty.

Victoria   We understand that it is very hot in India.

We never visited a tropical country you know.

Abdul   That is a great pity, ma'am. If you had but visited there once, the heavens would have showered the land with rose petals. That is how blessed we would have been with your presence – ma'am.

Victoria *smiles.*

Lady Sarah *does not like the Indian's flamboyancy.*

Victoria   Tell us about your city. Agra?

Abdul   It is a very beautiful city, ma'am.

Victoria *(impatient)*   . . . and?

Abdul *is unsure how much to speak.*

Abdul   Of course, it is dominated by the Red Fort and the Taj Mahal, built by the Mughal Emperor Shah Jahan. In memory of his beloved wife Mumtaz. A monument to the most highest love, between a man and a woman.

Lady Sarah *looks uncomfortable.*

Victoria   Our late husband, Albert, was fascinated by the stonework of the Taj Mahal. He would spend hours poring over portraits and sketches of the building.

Lady Sarah   I have seen sketches too.

Abdul   But you have not really 'seen it' until you have stood before it.

Victoria   Do describe it to us.

Abdul   My words cannot do it justice. In English . . .

Victoria   Try.

Abdul   It is breathtaking, overwhelming.

Victoria   And how does it make one feel when one gazes upon it?

Abdul   It feels like . . . forgive me, this is difficult to put into words . . .

Victoria   Please, in your own time.

Abdul *searches for the words.*

Abdul   It feels, it feels . . . As if Allah himself is watching over us.

Filling the air with love and reminding us why we are put on this earth . . . almost *not* a building of stone and marble, more a dream floating enticingly, perfectly in one's line of vision.

Lady Sarah   The Emperor must have loved his wife very much.

Abdul   She was his favourite wife and he was devastated when she died.

Lady Sarah   Giving birth to her fourteenth child I understand?

Abdul   It is said that Emperor Shah Jahan's hair went completely white overnight and that he went into mourning for two years.

Lady Sarah (*barbed*)   Only two . . .?

Victoria   Is it true that it changes colour according to the time of day?

Abdul *pours* **Victoria** *some tea. She looks at him eagerly.*

Abdul   Yes, ma'am.

Victoria   It must be a most extraordinary vision.

Abdul   It *was* more extraordinary than it is now. I'm afraid your soldiers, ma'am, and officials have chiselled out the precious stones so now . . .

Victoria   They are all gone?

Abdul   Yes. Looters over the years have stolen the carpets, jewels, silver doors and embroidered tapestries. My father says that when he was a boy English men and women used it as a pleasure resort, dancing on the terrace. May I?

Abdul *puts out his hands to* **Victoria**. *She takes his hand coquettishly and he pulls her up in a gentle waltz around the room.* **Lady Sarah** *stands, outraged.*

Lady Sarah   Ma'am! I must insist!

Victoria   Oh do hush, Sarah.

Abdul *dances gently with* **Victoria** *around the room.* **Lady Sarah** *stands and watches in horror.* **Victoria** *is like a giggly schoolgirl, hanging on* **Abdul***'s every word.*

Victoria   What happened to the Emperor? Wasn't there some sadness at the end of his life?

Abdul   There are stories that he planned to build an identical black marble mausoleum for himself on the other side of the river, which would be joined by a bridge. But he was unable to bring his plans to fruition. His son Aurangzeb led a coup and seized power. He imprisoned the old Emperor in the Red Fort where he died.

Victoria   How tragic. To be treated in such a manner by one's own blood!

Abdul   You can still see that in Shah Jahan's quarters where he was imprisoned, small mirrors were inlaid into the wall so that he was surrounded by thousands of reflections of his Taj Mahal. Like stars in the sky.

Victoria   Like stars in the sky.

Abdul   He was carried over the river after his death where even today he lies alongside his Queen Mumtaz.

Victoria   For all eternity.

Abdul *stops dancing and guides* **Victoria** *back to her seat. She is quite overcome.*

Lady Sarah *looks at* **Abdul** *suspiciously.*

Scene Eight

It is early morning and we are back at the Tilbury docks.

Firoza, *an Indian woman in her late thirties, is sat at the docks. She has a large bag and is eating a piece of bread. She is dressed in a black Victorian dress/uniform of an ayah and is cuddling a baby. She is humming a song and is of a very cheerful and slightly eccentric disposition.*

Rani *enters. She looks a little dishevelled and worried. She paces.* **Firoza** *watches for a while and then calls out.*

Firoza   Hey! Girlie!

Rani *stops and turns.* **Firoza** *smiles and waves at her.* **Rani** *approaches her.*

Firoza   Good morning!

Rani *nods.*

Firoza   Lost your way?

Rani   I am . . . yes . . . I . . .

Firoza   Come and sit down. Don't be frightened.

She pats the space on the bench next to her.

Rani *looks relieved.*

Firoza   First – introductions – Firoza Begum, from Nagpur.
(*She salaams.*) And you?

Rani   Rani Das – from Calcutta. (*She does namaste.*)

Firoza   You looking for work?

Rani   My family dismissed me – after the voyage over. They
promised me a position and then . . .

Firoza   Happens too often I'm afraid.

She puts her arm around **Rani** *and offers her some bread.*

Firoza   Go on – eat. It's a bit stale but 'least it's something in
your belly.

Rani (*takes some bread*)   You are very kind. Thank you.

Firoza   So, what happens next, little Rani?

Rani   They said they'd given me enough money for a passage
home – but when I went to try and buy a ticket . . .

Firoza   It wasn't enough.

Rani *looks distraught.*

Rani   I wish I could swim back.

Firoza *laughs heartily.* **Rani** *can't help but smile.*

Firoza   That's a good one – swim – eh? Too far to swim, can't
pay for your passage – where have you been staying?

Rani   A sailor took me to a place called Lascar Sally's last night.

Firoza   Lascar Sally? How is she?

Rani   She seemed . . . rough.

Firoza   She's a good woman. Has a tendency to get a bit too involved with those rascally lascars. I think she's rather partial to a bit of brown skin.

Rani   It's a horrid place.

Firoza   A bit rowdy . . . and filthy . . . and full of rats.

No place for a nice young girl. This sailor . . . did he . . . are you alright?

Rani *nods.*

Firoza   That's a relief. I've slept out in the open here before. Twenty years ago. Some of those English employers – morals of a ten-headed demon. After all – they're a nation of slave runners. It's in their blood. I think it's different from ours – cold . . .

Rani   Have you lived here for twenty years?

Firoza   I come and go. I'm about to set sail again.

Been working for an engineer's family in Hampstead for the last year. He's just got a job in Calcutta and I'm escorting his family back.

The baby in her arms starts to whimper. She rocks the baby.

Rani (*disappointed*)   Oh. Leaving today?

Firoza   In an hour.

Rani   Everything is so strange here! The cold, the streets, the people . . .

Firoza   The people are alright. Just got to get to know their ways.

Rani   This morning I thought I might die here.

Firoza   Don't speak like that.

Rani   You think people like me can survive in this city?

Firoza   You can not only survive but flourish! Make your own destiny.

Rani *looks hopeful.*

Rani   As I was coming here I looked into people's faces. They looked back at me with such coldness. Some of them laughed at me.

Firoza   They are not used to seeing your dress, that's all.

Rani   I kept wondering how I could become friends with them. I have so many questions that I would like answered.

Firoza   Questions?

Rani   The street lamps! How are they lit? They look so pretty in the dark, like misty stars. Where are the stables for the horses that pull the carriages? Are there any fruit here? Bananas? Mangoes?

Firoza   This is what you have to do.

You have to be brave, be bold and approach people and say: 'Excuse me, ma'am, I am an experienced ayah. I am looking for work.

I can dress hair, cook plain victuals. I am looking for service. I can wash well and will endeavour to make myself useful to any lady.' Understand?

Woman (*offstage*)   Firoza! Are you still alive!

Rani *nods.*

Firoza   Make sure you curtsey a lot. They like that.

It shows deference.

Woman (*offstage*)   Firoza!

Firoza   And go back to Lascar Sally's if you need to stay overnight. It may be dirty, but she has a heart of gold.

She expertly ties the baby in a sling around her.

(*To the baby.*) There you go – all snug now?

She gets up and picks up her bag.

I am sorry to leave you like this. But I must go.

She embraces **Rani**.

Firoza   Have faith in yourself.

She bustles off. **Rani** *remains seated for a while and then she produces a comb from her bag and combs her hair. She smooths her sari down and gets up when she sees an English woman passing by.*

Rani   Excuse me, ma'am . . . I am looking for work . . .

Woman One   No I am not looking for a servant . . .

Rani   I can dress hair, cook plain victuals, make bread . . .

The **Woman** *walks away.* **Rani** *tries to stop another English woman.*

Rani   Ma'am – I am a native of Bengal and I want a place as a servant to a family.

Woman Two   What happened to your last job?

Rani   I did not leave her place for any fault, but because it no longer suited the lady to keep me.

The **Woman** *shakes her head and walks away.* **Rani** *approaches another woman.*

Rani   Please . . . lady . . . ma'am, I need work . . .

Woman Three   You from India?

Rani   I lost my last job . . . I was hoping to work my passage back home.

Woman Three   You and every other black woman 'round here. Dunno why you all come in the first place. Why'd your mistress dismiss you?

Rani   She . . . she . . .

Woman Three   Threw you over? Fickle lot those toffs. I'm sorry I can't help you. Looking for work myself. Good luck though, love.

Rani *watches the woman as she approaches a group of sailors. They all look her up and down.* **Rani** *watches the* **Woman** *as she walks off with one of the sailors arm in arm.*

Rani *sits by the dockside and looks out to sea mournfully. She watches as people go by. Time passes. An English woman* (**Georgina**) *approaches* **Rani**. *She seems in a rush.*

Georgina   Excuse me, young lady . . . do you speak English?

Rani *stands and curtseys.*

Rani   Yes, ma'am.

Georgina   Well, at least that's a start. Are you an ayah?

Rani   Yes, ma'am.

Georgina   What is your name?

Rani   Rani.

Georgina   Rani? That's easy enough.

I understand you are looking for work?

The others told me. My mistress has lost her nanny. Stupid girl went and got herself in the family way and I had to dismiss her. I need someone to start work immediately.

Rani   You have children who need looking after?

Georgina   Yes . . . but they're not mine . . . my mistress's, you understand? Four little 'uns. Very spirited but well behaved. I am the housekeeper.

Rani   I see.

Georgina   My mistress always favours an Indian ayah.

Says you people are more obedient, don't mess around with men and that you are good with children.

Are you good with children?

Rani   Yes, ma'am.

Georgina   Do you have references?

Rani   Yes, ma'am.

She eagerly produces her references from her dress.

Georgina   Well, let's have a look at you. Stand up straight.

She makes **Rani** *stand in front of her and she has a good look at her eyes and her face; she walks around her and appraises her.*

Georgina   Age?

Rani   Sixteen.

Georgina   Constitution?

Rani   Erm?

Georgina   You're not sickly or anything?

Rani   No, I am strong and I can dress hair, cook plain victuals, make bread . . . wash well and will endeavour to make myself useful to you and the children . . .

Georgina   Can you cook curry?

Rani   Yes . . . if it is your wish . . .

Georgina   Not my wish – my master's.

Rani   I can cook curry.

Georgina   You'll do. Trial period for a month. You get paid at the end of the week. And you'll have your own bed in the servants' quarters.

My name is Georgina Philpott.

Rani   Yes, ma'am.

Georgina   But you can call me Georgie. Everyone does.

Rani   Yes. Yes. Oh! Thank you . . . thank you, Georgie.

May I ask – who will be my employers?

Georgina   Lord and Lady Oakham. Well, come along then.

Rani *follows* **Georgina** *as they both exit.*

Hari *comes running up, in a panic.*

Hari   RANI! RANI!

He looks around him wildly, out of breath.

Where is she?

(*Calls again.*) Rani! Rani?!

Serang *enters.*

Serang (*mimics* **Hari**)   Rani! Rani!

Hari   Ali . . . I've lost Rani.

Serang   Ahh . . . the girl that got away. Safe from your filthy clutches at least. She open her legs for you last night?

Hari   She isn't like that.

Serang   Yes, but *you* are like that.

Hari   You don't understand. She'll be lost. She needs help.

Serang   I'm sure she will survive and even thrive without you.

Hari   She won't.

He is distressed.

What have I done? I was useless. I should have been . . .

Serang *sniffs* **Hari**.

Serang   Filthy rascal. You stink of cheap gin . . . if you ask me, the girl had a lucky escape. Now follow me. The ship is loading now.

Hari   I can't, I have to find her.

Serang   You are turning down work?

Hari   No, it's just . . .

Serang   If you refuse to come with me immediately, I will make sure that no other captain or serang will give you employment ever again.

Hari   Please, Serang Ali, just give me one more day.

Serang *swears under his breath in Hindi.*

Serang   Let me remind you that you are under contract with the Clan Line. You must report to work now not chase after some bit of young skirt.

He turns and gives **Hari** *a hard look.* **Hari** *has no choice.* **Serang** *pushes and thumps* **Hari** *on.* **Hari** *looks back forlornly one last time, follows* **Serang** *and exits.*

Scene Nine

London.

Georgina *is dressing* **Rani** *in an English dress/uniform of a nanny.*

Rani's *hair is pinned up tidily.*

Georgina   You have such a lovely figure. And you suit this dress very nicely. It's a bit sombre, I know . . .

Rani *lifts her dress to examine her petticoat beneath.*

Rani   Such pretty petticoats.

Georgina   Oh Lordy! You mustn't go around showing off your petticoats!

Rani *swishes around the room in delight in her dress.*

Georgina   Come back child! (*She laughs.*)

Rani   I feel like dancing in this.

Georgina   I have to put this apron on you.

Rani   Do I look English?

Georgina *holds up a white pinny.*

Georgina   Hurry up! The master will be waiting for his dinner.

Rani   Do these shoes make me walk funny?

She allows **Georgina** *to tie the apron around her waist.*

Georgina   Lordy, such a tiny waist! Now, remember, the master is very formal so always be polite and address him as 'my lord'. And for goodness' sake, don't prattle on, asking him dozens of questions like you usually do.

Rani   I can't believe I've been here two weeks and haven't seen him yet.

Georgina (*hushed*)   Always at his club. Barely sees the children. Gentlemen have an easy life if you ask me. Now stand back and let's have a look at you.

Rani *stands obediently whilst* **Georgina** *fusses around her.*

Georgina   You've cooked all the dishes he asked for?

Rani   Yes, Georgie. Cook was a bit annoyed with me though.

Georgina   Never mind her. She's a bad-tempered old goat at the best of times.

Rani   Kept complaining about the smell.

Georgina   It *is* quite pungent.

Rani   It's the spices. You must try some yourself.

Georgina   Now don't take offence, but it's not really to my liking. The smell. The colour of the food looks all wrong to me. Can't tell what's what on the plate.

Rani   I'm a good cook.

Georgina   I'm sure you are. But the point is, you're cooking for the master. Not for me.

Lord John Oakham *calls.*

Lord Oakham (*offstage*)   Georgie! Where's the new girl?

Georgina   Coming, Your Lordship!

Lord Oakham (*offstage*)   I'm famished. Send her in at once.

Georgina   You'd better go. Good luck.

Rani *picks up the tray of food and carries it through.*

Scene Ten

During the following scene we see **Hari** *exhausted and lying in a small cramped space. He writes by the light of a candle on a ship somewhere out at sea.*

Lord Oakham *is sat at a table. There are an array of plates, cutlery and curries in front of him.* **Rani** *is serving him.* **Lord Oakham** *is watching her carefully.*

Lord Oakham   Tell me what you are serving me, Rani.

Rani   This one is . . .

Lord Oakham   No, let me guess . . .

He sniffs the food and takes a mouthful.

Hmmmm . . .

Aloo gobi.

Rani *smiles and nods. She serves another one. He tastes.*

Lord Oakham   Chicken . . . korma.

He eats.

It is a shame your mistress refuses to eat with me. She tells me the smell makes her nauseous.

Rani   It is not to her taste, my lord.

Lord Oakham   She was not brought up with this food as I was.

My ayah Jamila weaned me on rice and every day she would cook for me.

Rani *stands back at some distance.*

Rani   Shall I leave you, my lord?

Lord Oakham   What? And leave me to eat on my own? No!

Rani *looks bemused.*

Lord Oakham   Please, sit down. Stay with me until I have eaten.

Rani *sits down obediently.*

Lord Oakham   Delicious. Georgie did well to find you. Tell me, my girl, how are you settling in here?

Rani   Both you and the mistress have been very kind to me.

Lord Oakham   And your quarters?

Rani   Very comfortable, my lord.

Lord Oakham   Good. The children already seem to adore you, particularly my little Emily. You have fitted in to our little family seamlessly.

Rani *nods.*

Lord Oakham   You have no idea what a treat it is to find an Indian woman who can cook for me. Brings back so many happy memories for me. Freedom, no responsibilities and beauty all around me.

He looks at **Rani** *and smiles secretly.*

Lord Oakham   I have been fussing poor old cook to make me curry for years . . . she tried but never succeeded in creating anything as authentic as this.

I grew up in India you know – until the age of fourteen when I was sent back for my schooling.

Rani   You never went back, my lord?

Lord Oakham   Unfortunately not.

I will pay you a little extra, my girl, to cook for me every day except for Sundays. I know it may be a little tiring for you after your long day with the children, but it gives me such pleasure to eat the food of my childhood. You are agreeable to this?

Rani   It would give me great pleasure, my lord.

Lord Oakham   If you need more spices, then you must make a list and I shall pass it on to my man in the colonial offices. He is in charge of shipping produce and spices from the East so it is fairly easy for me to get hold of.

Rani   Thank you, my lord.

Lord Oakham   Thank *you*, Rani. Do you not have any clothing with you?

Rani   My lord?

Lord Oakham   I notice you are wearing that rather dull uniform. Don't you wear saris?

Rani   I have a couple with me, but Georgie thought it more appropriate that I should wear the dress of this country.

Lord Oakham   Perhaps when you're with the children – but I prefer to see you dressed as an Indian woman.

Rani *nods.*

Lord Oakham   It reminds me of my time in India.

Rani   As you wish, my lord.

Lord Oakham   And I want to hear all about your village back in India. What you did, where you grew up, your family . . . everything.

Rani   I'm afraid my lord will not find it very interesting.

Lord Oakham   Let me be the judge of that, my girl.

He sits back expectantly.

Rani   I come from a small village in Bengal.

Lord Oakham   Describe your village to me.

Rani   Small houses made from clay and mud. Very clean, hot . . . my father was a farmer, my mother an ayah for the Matthews family.

In the mornings, after I completed my chores, I would make my way to school. I would have to walk along the ridges that stretched between the paddy fields. Lush green, water shimmering on the surface – so green, sometimes it hurt your eyes. I would see water buffaloes lounging and basking in the big lakes, and once I spotted a tiger lapping water at the riverside.

Lord Oakham   Your parents sent you to school? That is unusual is it not?

Rani   My father wanted me to be educated. He saved all his money to buy me books.

Lord Oakham   A little more of the aloo gobi.

Rani *jumps up to serve more.*

Lord Oakham   Do you have a sweetheart, Rani?

Rani *looks embarrassed.*

Lord Oakham   Ahhh . . . there is someone isn't there?

Suddenly he takes **Rani**'s *face in his hands.*

Lord Oakham   How could such a beautiful, sweet creature not have at least a dozen admirers? Is there no one to look after you?

Rani   I do not need looking after, my lord.

Lord Oakham   Every woman needs the protection and admiration of a man. There must be someone . . .?

Rani *remains silent.*

Lord Oakham   Whoever he is, he is not worthy of you. You look so lost and lonely. No one in this country who understands you. No one to call a friend. Isolated, abandoned, frightened, so far away from home.

You are a hidden gem. Your eyes sparkle with something . . . knowing.

Rani   My Lord – please.

Lord Oakham   I could be a very good friend to you.

Rani   My lord?

Lord Oakham   If you were mine, I would know how to treat you . . . like a goddess.

Rani *looks at* **Lord Oakham***, perplexed.*

Lord Oakham *kisses* **Rani** *on the lips. She looks afraid.*

Rani   This is not right, my lord.

Lord Oakham *strokes* **Rani***'s hair.*

Lord Oakham   You are so lovely. Let me look after you, care for you . . . I can make your life here with us very comfortable. Eiderdowns to keep you warm, an allowance for your dresses and . . .

Rani   I need to send money orders back to India to my mother and brother.

Lord Oakham   Of course.

He kisses **Rani** *again. This time she kisses back, more passionately. He then pushes her gently down on to the couch. They start to make love.*

Hari *has finished his letter and reads it out to himself.*

Hari   My dearest Rani

It has been four months since I last saw you. My mind still goes back to that night and how I let you down so badly. I wanted to help and instead, I was a weak man who acted dishonourably towards you.

I took your advice and am learning my letters in the hope of finishing off what you inspired me to do.

I keep myself strong so that maybe one day I will see you again.

I will send these words to Lascar Sally and hope that they will eventually find you. I love you, Rani, and I hope you will forgive the stupidity of a wretched and unformed lascar. I pray for your well-being and that I will see you again.

Your friend always, Hari.

Scene Eleven

Victoria *is sitting on a chair, dressed for a royal occasion. (Party noises in the background. Chamber music.) She is holding court to* *a party but looks very tired and worn.* **Abdul** *is standing next to her, holding a tray with a glass on it.* **Victoria** *intermittently takes a drink and replaces the glass on the tray. She waves her hand around towards the audience to indicate the guests.*

Victoria   All our subjects from all the corners of our Empire, come to see their Queen and Sovereign.

Abdul *looks into the crowd obviously amazed.*

Abdul   Ma'am, you are the most powerful and respected monarch in the world.

Might I ask, when will you make it official?

Victoria   You are too impatient, Abdul.

Abdul   There is whispering and gossip at court that Your Majesty treats me as one would an exotic pet.

Victoria   Ahh . . . but a beloved pet.

She laughs.

Abdul   Your Majesty enjoys my discomfort at these words?

Victoria   We enjoy having you by our side.

Abdul   I am your loyal servant but there are those out there who do not trust me. If you were to make the appointment official, I would not have to suffer the indignities of being ridiculed, ma'am.

Victoria   Come, come, Abdul. There are procedures we must adhere to.

Abdul   You gave me your word.

Victoria   Are you questioning our word, Abdul?

Abdul   No, ma'am, I apologize. I am simply eager to serve you to the best of my abilities.

Victoria   Bertie asked us if you were trustworthy.

Abdul   Ma'am?

Victoria   If you have any connections with Indian agitators?

She looks at **Abdul***.*

Victoria   Well? Have you? Any connections that is?

Abdul (*affronted*)   With all due respect to His Royal Highness I find that questioning of my character, extremely . . . insulting . . .

Victoria *laughs.* **Abdul** *looks even more affronted.*

Victoria   There are people out there who have tried to assassinate us you know.

Abdul   Ma'am . . . I am so sorry for the suffering that has caused you . . . but to think . . . that I would attempt to hurt or conspire against Your Majesty in any way . . . pains me to the core of my heart . . .

Victoria   We have told Bertie you are harmless.

Abdul   If Your Majesty wishes to dismiss me from her service, or if Your Majesty feels that I am unworthy of such office, close to your royal person . . .

Victoria *waves* **Abdul***'s concerns away.*

Victoria   Abdul – please.

She takes a sip of water.

Abdul   Ma'am, I am keen to communicate the news to my father in Agra . . . he is an old man now . . .

Victoria   We are to travel to Balmoral next week for the summer. You will be commanded to attend Abdul.

Abdul *bows.*

Victoria   We have asked our men up there to make you comfortable in the rooms on the first floor. They are particularly excellent rooms with a view of the grounds.

Abdul   My eternal gratitude, ma'am.

Victoria   They used to belong to our beloved keeper . . .

Abdul   I am sorry to press the point but when will you . . .?

Victoria *smiles at* **Abdul** *coquettishly.*

Victoria   It is already done.

Abdul *looks confused.*

Victoria   We have arranged it and it is official. We wish to raise you from the role of *khitmagar* to that of *munshi.* Instead of cooking curries, you will be our teacher.

You will forthwith be relieved of such menial tasks as waiting at the table.

Abdul   May I ask that all the photographs which have been taken of me handing dishes to you will be destroyed. These are quite beneath my dignity.

Victoria   It shall be done. Go and write to your father in Agra and add that we wish to commission Von Angeli to do a portrait of you.

Abdul   Thank you, ma'am.

He smiles and bows deeply. He calls over another servant.

Servant *approaches.*

Abdul   I am no longer a waiter. Please take my tray.

The confused **Servant** *looks at* **Victoria** *who nods. He takes the tray from* **Abdul**'s *hands and stands in place of* **Abdul** *by the Queen's side.*

Servant *bows to* **Victoria** *and* **Abdul** *stands close by on the other side of her. He looks proud.*

Scene Twelve

Hari *on the boat. He is working hard with other* **Lascars***. A storm is raging and they are stacking cargo onto a boat. The work is back-breaking.* **Hari** *looks ragged and tired.*

Serang *surveys the work.*

They sing a mournful song as they work.

('Eki Dumah' – lascar song)
Kay, kay, kay, kay!
Eki dumah!
Kay, kay, kay, kay!
Eki dumah!
Somerset akilla coolie man
Eki dumah!
Somerset akilla Bosun's mate
Eki dumah!
Somerset akilla wirefall
Eki dumah!
Somerset akilla coolie man
Kay, kay, kay, kay!
Eki dumah!
Kay, kay, kay, kay!
Eki dumah!
Kay, kay, kay, kay!
Eki dumah!
Kay, kay, kay, kay!
Eki dumah!
Sailorman no likee Bosun's mate
Eki dumah!
Bosun's mate no likee Head Serang
Eki dumah!
Head Serang no likee Number One
Eki dumah!
Number One no likee coolie man,
Kay, kay, kay, kay!
Eki dumah!
Kay, kay, kay.

*As **Hari** is working hard on the boat, we see **Rani** working too.
She is with four children, playing, feeding, etc. We see that she is
heavily pregnant.*

*We also see **Dadabhai** busy with papers, sat behind a desk. He is
meeting with a respectable-looking Englishman. They shake hands
and greet each other animatedly and sit down to talk.*

Scene Thirteen

Osborne House.

Lady Sarah *is sitting outside in the sunshine with* **Victoria**.

Victoria *is seated at a desk, writing.*

Lady Sarah   I have met the Munshi's wife.

Victoria *stops writing. She tries to hide her jealousy.* **Lady Sarah** *watches her carefully.*

Victoria   What does she look like?

Lady Sarah   She is fat and not uncomely, a delicate shade of chocolate and gorgeously attired, rings on her fingers, rings in her nose, a pocket mirror set in turquoises on her thumb and every feasible part of her person hung with chains and bracelets and earrings.

She had a rose pink veil on her head bordered with heavy gold and splendid silk and satin swathings around her person. It all seemed so . . . so . . . un-English . . .

Victoria   She is essentially oriental.

Lady Sarah   Doctor Reid has pointed out something slightly indelicate about the Munshi.

Victoria   How so?

Lady Sarah   He has been to visit Mrs Karim on a few occasions now and whilst he is not allowed to see his patient's face, he is expected to diagnose simply by looking at the lady's tongue.

Victoria   The woman of the household is not permitted to reveal her form to any man other than her husband. She remains veiled. That is the custom.

Lady Sarah   Forgive me, ma'am, but there is some question as to exactly how many Mrs Karims there are.

It seems that whenever Dr Reid is asked to attend Mrs Karim, a different tongue is put out to him to examine.

Victoria   That is Abdul's business, not ours. We do not interrogate him on his private affairs.

Lady Sarah   But surely, ma'am, it is not morally proper to encourage a servant to live in some kind of a harem with an exotic menagerie?

Victoria   He is not a servant – please never refer to Abdul as such. He is our teacher. He will also teach us something about the religions and customs of India. It is of great interest to us for both the language and the people – we have never naturally come into real contact with before.

Lady Sarah   Ma'am, when he returns to India . . .

Victoria   He is simply going on vacation. He has served us loyally for three years now and it is only proper that he should once in a while visit his family.

Lady Sarah   I hope you will see fit to distance yourself a little from him, whilst he is away.

Victoria   What is your meaning?

Lady Sarah   Ma'am . . . the rumours and whisperings at court are not very tasteful.

Victoria   You mean there's gossip about us? At our age? How entertaining. What exactly are they saying?

Lady Sarah   Members of your court say, you are showing undue favouritism towards the Indian. They fear . . . the Munshi is exploiting Her Majesty.

That he almost thinks of himself as royalty and they are resenting his constant presence by your side . . . Ma'am . . . And Lord Ponsonby says that Abdul's father is not a surgeon in the Indian army, or anything of the sort. He is a hospital assistant in Agra jail with no medical diploma.

Victoria   That is preposterous! They either found the wrong man or they decided to invent a little fiction.

Lady Sarah   They also say that he has a friend – a Rafiuddin Ahmed . . .

Victoria   Yes, he is studying at the Bar here.

Lady Sarah   The Home Office have their eye on this man and believe him to be an untrustworthy adventurer in contact with disorderly elements both here and in India.

Victoria   I have met Mr Ahmed and I can assure you, he is a most educated and pleasant young man.

Lady Sarah (*horrified*)   You have met him? I must warn you ma'am. Ahmed is a member of the Indian League here in Britain along with another man who goes by the most ridiculous name – Dadabhai Naoroji.

Victoria   It is a Parsi name. And I have heard of this Naoroji too. I made Lord Salisbury apologize to him for calling him a 'black man'.

Lady Sarah   Then you must know that this Parsi intends to stand as a Member of Parliament. He is gathering support. Perhaps it would be wise to distance yourself from anyone who has links with Indian Home Rule.

Victoria   Enough! We *will* have our Munshi.

Lady Sarah *bows in deference but she is upset.*

Scene Fourteen

Outside **Lord Oakham**'s *house. We see two bundles of clothes being thrown out onto the street. Then* **Rani** *is pushed roughly out.*

Lord Oakham *is standing on the back steps of his house.*

Rani *stands below him on the street, her belongings all around her, heavily pregnant. She is distraught and crying.*

She looks careworn and slightly ragged, her hair dishevelled. **Georgina** *stands in the background and watches on in horror.*

Lord Oakham　You and your damned lies.

Rani　Lies?!

Lord Oakham　You told the mistress. You told her a gross untruth – and now she has taken to her bed. That I cannot forgive. You are to leave immediately.

Rani　But the children . . . Little Emily . . . she will be heartbroken . . .

Lord Oakham　She will get over it. You are a harlot.

Rani　I am carrying your child.

Lord Oakham　No! It is not mine!

Rani　You were the only man who touched me!

Lord Oakham　Keep your voice down, you whore. Trying to trick me.

Rani　You promised to protect and care for me!

Lord Oakham　I promised you nothing.

Rani　What about the baby?

Lord Oakham　Shut your mouth before I have to shut it myself.

Georgina *rushes forward to try and protect* **Rani**.

Georgina　My lord, we can't just throw the girl out onto the streets. How will she provide for her baby?

Lord Oakham　Georgie, you stay out of this.

Georgina　Give her a few days to find somewhere else.

Rani　Where will I go?

Lord Oakham　Rani, I don't care. I have no interest in knowing what becomes of you and your bastard child. Put her in the workhouse when she is born. Leave her on the steps. She can join the ranks of other bastard children all over the city. Or better still, drown her.

Rani　You monster! You can have anything and still you take?

She picks up clods of earth and starts flinging them in a blind rage at **Lord Oakham**.

Lord Oakham   Stop it!

Georgina   Oh Rani – be careful!

Rani   Destroyed everything – hopes, dreams, future . . . and you made a fool of me.

Lord Oakham   I'm warning you . . .

Rani   You can call me a liar, but your wife knows you're a snake. She knows.

Lord Oakham (*to* **Rani**)   Get away from here or I will call my men.

Lord Oakham *storms back into the house.* **Georgina** *looks at* **Rani** *helplessly. She helps pick up her clothes for her and hands them back.*

Georgina   You girls. I try to help but you never learn.

Rani   You brought me here, Georgie.

Georgina   Yes, but I expected you to have some self-respect.

Rani   Did you find the last nanny for the Oakhams? Didn't she have a baby too? What about the one before that?

Georgina   You're not suggesting . . .?

Rani *looks at* **Georgina** *fiercely.* **Georgina** *looks horrified as the penny drops*

Georgina   Oh Lordy.

Lord Oakham (*offstage*)   Georgie! Come back in at once

Rani *leaves, destitute.* **Georgina** *watches her go – distressed.*

Scene Fifteen

Abdul *is teaching* **Victoria** *Hindi.*

We also see **Rani** *holding a newborn baby.*

Abdul   *Namaste.*

Victoria   *Namaste.*

Abdul   I am delighted to make your acquaintance.

Victoria (*repeats in Hindi*)   *Hame tum se mil ker bohut khushi hui.*

Abdul   Remember to use the formal address of you as in '*aap*'.

Victoria (*in Hindi*)

Aap ko hamari garmi kesi lagi. Yehe din bohut lambe he.

(How are you enjoying our summer? The days are very long in July.)

Abdul   Excellent, ma'am. Your pronunciation is almost perfect.

Victoria *giggles like a child.*

Victoria   We want to learn how to say 'Good luck with your voyage'.

Abdul   We must not run before we can walk, ma'am.

Victoria   Pardon?

Abdul   You still have to write that first sentence.

Victoria   You are a hard taskmaster, Abdul.

She grumbles under her breath and starts writing.

Abdul *strolls around as* **Victoria** *writes.*

Victoria   We have written to Lord Lansdowne to grant you some land in Agra. When you go back, you must identify the land and write me the details.

Abdul   Thank you, ma'am. I am forever in your debt.

Victoria   We will die before you, Abdul, and when we do, we want to make sure that you and your family are provided for.

Abdul   Please, ma'am, do not speak of death. I am your devoted servant and it pains me most severely to think of a world without you.

Abdul *falls to his knees and kisses* **Victoria**'s *hand.*

Victoria   We will be at a great loss without you.

Abdul   It is only for a while, my Sovereign.

Victoria   Please take good care of yourself.

Abdul   I will.

Victoria   How does one say 'I love you' in Hindi?

Abdul *hesitates and looks at* **Victoria**.

Abdul   Ma'am . . .

Victoria   Tell me.

Abdul (*in Hindi*)

Me tum se pyar karti hui.

(I love you.)

Victoria (*in Hindi*)

Me tum se pyar karti hui.

With all my heart. And I will count the days until you return safely to England.

She reaches out, takes the Munshi's hand and kisses it.

We see **Rani** *wandering, sobbing, clutching her baby.*

She reaches the docks, stops and looks out to sea. She cradles the baby.

Rani   I am sorry, little one. I cannot stay with you.

The baby cries. **Rani** *tries to hush her.*

Rani   I love you. But I am going away tonight. I am stuck here on the island, imprisoned on all sides by the grey churning seas – maybe without me . . . you have a chance.

She places the baby on the ground and walks away.

Act Two

NB: Throughout the second half of the play we see **Hari** *travelling around the Empire. These are visual representations of his work as a sailor.*

Scene One

Tilbury docks, 1891.

Sally *and* **Firoza** *are both standing at the docks.* **Sally** *is waving furiously and blowing kisses. (***Firoza** *has a bad leg and is walking with the aid of a stick.*)

Sally   Bye, love! I'll miss you, darlin'. Come back to me!

Firoza *doesn't look too impressed.*

Sally   I must stop doing this, Firoza. My poor heart's been broken so many times.

Firoza *is silently disapproving.*

Sally   Don't look at me like that.

Firoza   I said nothing.

Sally   Do you think he'll come back?

Firoza   He'll come back if he survives.

Sally   You really know how to cheer a girl up. My heart's been shattered, it has.

Firoza   Ha!

Sally (*protests*)   I love my Ganesh. Such a man!

Did you see those muscles of his?

Firoza   It was hard not to. Always challenging everyone to arm-wrestling competitions and then ripping off his shirt when he won.

Sally (*laughs at the memory*)   He's so strong. Built like a god.

Firoza *giggles.*

Sally   Why you laughing at me? What I'm feeling right now – the grief – it's real y'know.

Firoza *takes* **Sally**'s *hand and pats it.*

Firoza   I do not doubt your capacity to love, Sally. You have a very big heart.

Sally *sobs a little.* **Firoza** *looks on with empathy.*

Sally   Funny thing the sea. Always seems to call them back. However much they yearn for land – they always get itchy feet and want to get back out there. I don't get it myself.

Firoza   It's the adventure, the smell of new lands, of different people . . . the promise of something fresh.

Sally   It's an excuse not to settle down. I wonder if Ganesh had a wife and family back home?

Firoza *is silent.*

Sally   There's no fool like an old fool, eh – Firoza?

Firoza   Look!

Firoza *and* **Sally** *turn to see* **Rani** *who is standing a slight distance from her baby.* **Rani** *seems frozen in indecision.* **Firoza** *and* **Sally** *look on in horror at the baby on the ground.*

Sally   What's she doing? She's not . . .?

Firoza *motions at* **Sally** *to keep quiet and then they both approach* **Rani** *casually.*

Firoza   Oh! What a beautiful baby!

Rani *is silent.*

Sally   Gorgeous. So tiny! What is its name?

Rani *cannot look at* **Firoza** *and* **Sally** *in the eye.*

Firoza   May I?

Firoza *scoops the baby up in her arms and rocks her. She hums a lullaby.*

Firoza   Are you waiting for passage?

Rani   I don't want this baby. She is a curse on my life.

Firoza   Don't say that . . . look at her . . . she's perfect . . .

Sally   Some bloke got you in trouble and then dumped you? Promised you the world did he?

Rani   He said he loved me, that he'd protect me.

Firoza *expertly wraps the baby tight and rocks her.*

Firoza   You must learn to protect yourself.

Rani   It was better for both of us that I was dead!

Firoza   No. Don't speak like that.

Sally   A week from now and you'll feel differently.

Firoza   You don't remember me do you, girlie? It's me, Firoza. We met a few years ago at the docks.

Rani *looks at* **Firoza** *for the first time.*

Sally   You're the girl that Hari brought back. It's Sally.

Rani   I know who you are.

Firoza *carefully places the baby back in* **Rani***'s arms.*

Firoza   We should give the baby a name.

Rani   If my mother was here, she would have done that . . . in my village, it is always the grandmothers who name . . .

Firoza   I had a best friend when I was growing up called Asha. Do you like that name? It means 'Hope'.

Rani   I can never go back now. The shame, the dishonour.

Firoza *smiles and coos at the baby.*

Firoza   Hello, little Asha. How would you like to come and live with your mother and me? I live in a big house.

The baby stops crying.

There, you see? She likes that idea.

Rani   Please, look after my baby for me.

She yries to hand the baby over to **Firoza** *but she backs off.*

Firoza   She is yours.

Rani   No, no, you don't understand . . .

Firoza   I do understand. This is not the way.

Rani   Hari never came back for me . . . my master used me . . . I have no friends. . .I have been abandoned by everyone I ever met here.

Sally   I saw Hari a year ago. He was heading out to Africa on a ship carrying rail tracks. He was asking after you. He left a letter for you.

I got it back at the house. Come on. Never thought I'd see you again.

Firoza   You look exhausted. Come on. We'll curse the bad and praise the good.

Sally   It will make you feel so much better. Come.

Firoza *takes* **Rani** *by the arm,* **Sally** *puts her arm around her and together they lead* **Rani** *away.* **Rani** *walks slowly, as if in a daze. They exit together.*

Scene Two

On board a ship out at sea. **Hari** *is hammering up a large written notice. His fellow lascar crewmen crowd around him, worried.*

Hari *calls out to his fellow crewmen.*

Hari   Brothers, we shouldn't put up with these conditions. Day and night we toil and labour. We have to make demands and not allow ourselves to be treated like animals.

Lascar One   But Hari . . . we'll get into trouble. They'll punish us.

Lascar Two   They'll cut our food rations.

Hari   We're nearly starving to death as it is.

Lascar One   I don't even know what your notice says. I can't read.

Hari   The notice is for the captain. It says:

'Lascar demands:

1 Equal pay with the white sailors.
2 Equal food and water rations as the white sailors.
3 No more beatings by the first officer.
4 Rest periods between heavy labour.
But most of all
5 We demand to be respected as members of the human race.'

The other **Lascars** *all cheer.*

Scene Three

Jewry Street, Aldgate. Home for Ayahs, 1891.

We are outside a house. **Mary** *and* **Charlotte**, *two English women, dressed sombrely, are standing proudly before a banner, which reads 'Jewry Street, Aldgate. Home for Ayahs'.* **Dadabhai** *and a few Victorian ladies and gentlemen are also there. The scene opens with everyone singing a Christian hymn with great gusto.*

At the end of the hymn **Dadabhai** *steps forward and makes a speech.*

Dadabhai   After much lobbying by a committee of concerned British women (**Dadabhai** *bows in acknowledgement to the ladies*) we have finally secured this home. It will serve as a refuge for our beloved ayahs who have been ill-treated, dismissed from service or simply abandoned by the families which they have loyally served. We aim to find our ayahs placements with suitable families returning to India to end their suffering and to avoid starvation and deprivation.

Man (*calls out*)   Here! Here!

Bravo!

Mary   Thank you.

Thank you everyone for your support in making this venture finally happen.

Charlotte   Especially to our parliamentary candidate Dadabhai Naoroji who has striven tirelessly to make our dreams a reality.

Dadabhai *bows majestically.*

Mary   This home will be an expression of Christian charity for the welfare of Indian womanhood, representing the caring mother country binding the colonized in a web of gratitude and loyalty.

She ends her speech and everyone claps and cheers.

Charlotte   Now please, everyone, do come and have a look around the place.

The doors open and we see the inside of the Home for the Ayahs. In the drawing room, we see **Rani**, **Firoza** *and another couple of* **Ayahs** *sitting around the table, reading, sewing, embroidering, etc. Some are wearing saris with hair scraped back in buns, others are in the Victorian nanny's black outfit, whilst others wear traditional dress of their country.* **Rani** *is reading to a small child* (*Asha*). *All the* **Ayahs** *sit demurely, quietly and do not make any eye contact.*

Man   How interesting. How many women do you intend to house here?

Charlotte   At the moment, we have fifteen rooms, which means we can house up to forty – forty-five at a push.

Woman   As many as that?

Charlotte   We already have a waiting list of fifty ayahs, all destitute and unable to find accommodations, so as you can see the demand is there.

Mary   And that is why we intend to try and find work for these ladies. This will be a safe place for prospective employers to come and peruse the different ayahs, so that they can choose for themselves someone suitable for their family.

Charlotte   Let me introduce you to one of our ladies.

Firoza. (*Calls out.*) Firoza! Do come forward. Firoza, say hello to everyone.

Firoza   Good morning, ladies and gentlemen. Very pleased to make your acquaintance.

Mary   Firoza, do tell the ladies and gentlemen your story.

Firoza   I am an ayah – but I like boats. I like the smack of salty wind on my face, the sea breeze in my hair and the thunder of waves. I've rolled across those vast oceans back and forth forty times.

Man   Forty?!

Firoza   My mother always said I had itchy feet but to be honest, I never wanted to stay where I was mistreated.

Woman   Your mother mistreated you?

Firoza   My mother, my brothers, my husband. I was married at fourteen, a mother at fifteen, lost my baby to malaria when I was sixteen and my husband and family abused and blamed me. So I ran away from them all.

I looked after English families' children on the voyage over here from our country and then I would go back again. If I counted up how many children I looked after, I would say it was about two hundred.

Everyone gasps. A few people applaud her.

However, on my last voyage over there was a storm and a piece of ship's masonry fell on my leg. I was badly wounded and could no longer work. Back in London, I fell destitute. If it wasn't for

Mary and Charlotte finding me begging on the streets, I don't know what I would have done. They took me to a good doctor and my leg is healed now.

Everyone claps and cheers.

Charlotte   Now, ladies and gentlemen, a little stroll through the bedrooms and then on to the gardens?

As the ladies and gents all saunter off for a guided tour, the **Ayahs** *are all left on their own.*

Firoza   Did I perform well?

Rani   You should be on the stage.

The honourable ayah saved by charity and good works.

Firoza   I sounded like a mad pirate.

Rani   'The smack of salty wind on my face, the sea breeze in my hair.'

They fall about laughing. They get up from their demure occupations at the table and a couple of them run to the window to look outside.

Ayah   They'll be back in a moment!

Firoza   They'll be ages – oohing and aahing about the rooms, the gardens, the weeping willow . . . come on, we've waited for this day long enough.

Rani   A roof over our heads.

Firoza   A decent bed with a soft mattress. And coverlets.

Ayah   And clean washrooms.

Firoza *starts to sing a jaunty sea shanty. The others all sing along and dance.*

Ayah   Quick! They're coming back!

Everyone rushes back to their seats, picks up their embroidery, etc. and sit down in complete silence. **Charlotte** *re-enters with the* *ladies and gents. As they all troop in, they are all delighted with the tour.*

Woman   Excellent accommodation. Thank you for showing us around.

Man   Ladies, you are all very lucky.

Everyone starts to leave.

Dadabhai *turns to* **Rani**.

Dadabhai   I'd been standing here racking my brain, trying to work out where we met before and then suddenly it came back to me in a flash. You are the inquisitive ayah!

Rani   Inquisitive ayah?

Dadabhai   That's what myself and Gandhi nicknamed you. You spent the entire voyage asking everyone questions.

Rani   I'm sorry. I hope I wasn't a terrible bore.

Dadabhai   To the contrary, my dear. We both remarked on how it was a mark of intelligence.

I am sorry to learn that you had fallen on hard times. How have you managed these past few years?

Rani   I found friends who helped me . . . I went to evening classes . . . brushed up on my reading. I am alright now. It's good to see you, Dadabhai. I've read about you in the papers and I've even been to hear you speak a few times.

Dadabhai   Young lady. As your fellow countryman, I am very proud of your achievements. Keep up the good work.

He does a little bow and then turns to exit along with the others. **Rani** *calls out to him.*

Rani   Mr Naoroji . . . please wait . . .

Dadabhai *stops and turns.*

Rani   I know that you are campaigning to get into Parliament.

Dadabhai   Yes, my child.

Rani   I want to help you in your work – in any way I can.

Dadabhai   And how do you suppose you could help me?

Rani   By taking notes . . . of meetings . . . making appointments for you . . .

Dadabhai *looks at* **Rani** *long and hard.*

Dadabhai   You are interested in politics?

Rani   Yes.

Dadabhai   Why?

Rani   I want to help people who have fallen by the wayside. The poor and the destitute.

Dadabhai   Noble sentiments, Rani, but you should perhaps help the Church in their work. The ladies here would welcome it.

Rani   But I am not a Christian and I do not always agree with their methods.

Dadabhai   Ah ha! So you are a traitor to the cause.

Rani   No! I want to support your work to be the first Indian Member of Parliament. We need a voice in there. We are undervalued and treated as beneath the white man's concern. I know, from personal experience.

You said you were proud of me. I too am proud of you.

Beat as **Dadabhai** *appraises* **Rani**.

Dadabhai   Come to my house at noon tomorrow.

Let us see how accomplished you are. I expect hard workers and quick minds.

Rani   I can do it.

Dadabhai   I am not promising anything.

He gives **Rani** *his card with his address on it.*

Rani   Thank you, Dadabhai. I will be there.

Dadabhai *places his hand gently on* **Rani**'s *head and then exits.*

Dadabhai   'Til tomorrow my child!

Scene Four

Osborne House, 1891.

Victoria *is seated at a desk, writing, whilst* **Abdul** *is standing to one side in a pose. He is particularly well dressed in a flamboyantly tied turban. A* **Portrait Painter** *is painting him.* **Lady Sarah** *is standing by* **Victoria**'s *side handing her papers to sign or to read.*

Lady Sarah   Another letter from Cecil Rhodes.

Victoria   He's always writing to me.

Lady Sarah   He says here: 'I contend that we are the first race in the world and that the more of the world we inhabit the better it is for the human race.'

Victoria   He is indeed a most loyal and ardent servant.

And, of course, a very wealthy one.

Lady Sarah (*giggles*)   Mr Rhodes writes here that, if he could, he would annexe the planets in the sky for his Queen.

Victoria   He is rather too ardent.

Abdul   Excuse me, sir.

Painter   Yes?

Abdul   Might I make a small suggestion as regards this portrait?

Portrait Painter   Indeed.

Abdul   Given that I am Her Majesty's Munshi – her teacher you understand, rather than standing here empty-handed – would it not be more appropriate for me to be holding a book? I think it would more suitably convey the fact that I am a man of learning.

Portrait Painter   An excellent suggestion. Ma'am?

He looks across at **Victoria**.

Victoria   Lady Sarah, bring Abdul a gilt-edged book.

Lady Sarah *hides her emotions, curtseys and exits the room.*

Victoria   (*Calls out.*) And do make sure it isn't a Bible. How is the portrait coming on?

Portrait Painter   Favourably, ma'am.

Victoria   We wish to present it to our loyal servant Abdul by the time of his birthday in four months' time.

Portrait Painter   I have no doubt that I will be able to complete the task. (*To* **Abdul**.) Mr Karim, do please stay still.

Abdul   It is quite hard to keep in this position for prolonged periods.

Lady Sarah *re-enters and hands* **Abdul** *a book.*

Lady Sarah   Mr Karim is a young man of action and thus finds it hard to keep still in one place.

Portrait Painter   We will take a break in a while.

Abdul   Thank you, Lady Sarah.

Lady Sarah *looks at* **Abdul** *coldly and returns to her station by* **Victoria**.

Abdul   And perhaps a quill pen?

Portrait Painter   I think a book will suffice.

Abdul   A book without a pen seems a little . . . incomplete.

Victoria   Lady Sarah, here, please give this to Abdul to hold.

Victoria *takes a quill pen from her desk and hands it to* **Lady Sarah**. **Lady Sarah** *takes the pen across to* **Abdul**. *The* **Portrait Painter** *takes the pen and arranges* **Abdul** *in a pose with book and quill.*

Lady Sarah *returns to* **Victoria**'s *side.* **Victoria** *glances over a letter.*

Lady Sarah   And there has been some more progress in Uganda . . . our military administrator Lugard held firm against the Germans and the French in a battle over the four hills of Kampala.

Abdul   Thanks I believe to his possession of a Maxim machine gun, ma'am.

Lady Sarah   What is your meaning?

Abdul   Simply that many innocent lives must have been lost in a matter of hours. War brings terrible suffering, something you have never experienced, ma'am.

Victoria   We may be Queen and Empress but we are not made of stone. We can still feel for the suffering of our subjects. They are all our children.

Abdul   But feeling is not the same as experiencing, ma'am.

Lady Sarah *is furious.*

Lady Sarah (*to* **Abdul**)   I do not think it appropriate to have to listen to your audacious opinions on . . .

Victoria   Abdul is my teacher.

Lady Sarah   Of the Indian alphabet.

Victoria *raises her hand to stop* **Lady Sarah**.

Abdul   My apologies, Lady Sarah, I did not mean to show disrespect.

Lady Sarah   It is not to me you should be apologising but to our Queen.

Abdul   As a teacher, I cannot help but question things I notice.

Lady Sarah   As a servant of the Queen, you should know your boundaries.

Victoria   Please, will you both stop bickering?

Lady Sarah *glares at* **Abdul**.

Abdul   Ma'am, I am simply raising an interesting philosophical question. How is it that monarchs are able to remain human whilst their subjects suffer such great hardships?

Victoria *is silent.*

Abdul   You have no fear, you do not have to subject yourself to the daily humiliation of abuse. You are subservient to no one. Every day, as we speak, in Africa your subjects are gaining more land in your name. True, the Africans are not enslaved anymore but how can your power as a monarch be kept just and fair?

Victoria *is emotional. The* **Portrait Painter** *stops, slightly shocked at* **Abdul***'s nerve.*

Lady Sarah   Slavery has been abolished. The African people are free subjects of the British Crown. We are not gaining land through war, we are making treaties with the tribal leaders of those countries.

Abdul *bows to* **Lady Sarah**.

Lady Sarah   Her Majesty's duty is to bring light into darkness, the very essence of our country's destiny is to bring civilization to the world.

The **Portrait Painter** *busies himself with his brushes, slightly flustered.*

Abdul   Forgive me if I have spoken out of turn, ma'am.

Victoria   We are not blind to injustices. Our Christian beliefs are intended to spread harmony throughout the empire. It pains us to see our emissaries causing death and destruction in subjugating people.

We bring order to chaos. We are not in the habit of quelling nations through brutality. We do not seek to cause suffering.

Abdul   Ma'am, if only your agents and servants abroad were as high-minded as you are. Then the world would be a happier place.

He bows in deference but **Victoria** *is unnerved by the conversation. The* **Portrait Painter** *holds his nerve and continues to paint.* **Lady Sarah** *is stunned by* **Abdul**'s *audacity.*

Scene Five

NB: Somewhere during this scene/at the beginning we see **Hari** *being roughly carried off the ship by two fellow* **Lascars**. *He is beaten and bloodied.* **Serang** *stands over him as* **Hari** *is thrown to the ground.*

Serang   The captain does not want you on board his ship. He says you are a poisonous influence on your fellow seamen and a trouble maker.

Hari *groans in pain.*

Serang *helps* **Hari** *up. He looks back at the ship nervously.*

Serang   Go. Get away before the captain changes his mind and claps you in irons.

Hari   At least give me the name of the country you are leaving me in.

Serang   The Cape. This is where we part ways, Hari.

I wish you luck. Go well and succeed.

Serang *gives* **Hari** *one last look and exits.*

Rani *sits, shy and nervous in a drawing room.* **Dadabhai** *sits at his desk. He hands over a pamphlet to* **Rani**.

Dadabhai   Out loud please . . . I just want to see how well you can read. No point trying to help me in my work if you can't read. What is the title of the piece?

Rani   'The Heathen at Our Gate'.

Dadabhai   Very good. Do you know what a heathen is?

Rani   Someone who is not Christian?

Dadbhai   A derogatory, biblical term. Go on.

Rani *starts to read. At first nervously, stumbling over the words, and then more confidently.*

Rani   'There are at this moment estimated twenty-six Indian students of law attending our universities across the country. Groups of uncontrollable raw youth lacking self-control are roaming the streets at night. Considered unable to withstand the pressures of English society, these dark-skinned men easily succumb to the temptations of London life in particular. They find attractions of a London brothel (*She coughs apologetically.*) and intercourse with white women almost irresistible. Unlike their sisters in India the English woman here finds the Bengali Baboos captivating and rush at them willingly becoming their victims.'

Dadabhai   It is quite an epidemic.

Rani   Dada?

Dadabhai   Overrun by twenty-six young Indians. How awful. It's like the Vikings all over again.

He laughs uproariously at his own joke. **Rani** *watches him laugh and joins in.*

Dadabhai   Tell me, Rani, what have you read?

Rani   Novels mainly . . . Charles Dickens, Thackeray, Jane Austen, Brontës, Kipling . . .

Dadbhai   Kipling . . . hmmm . . . but very well-read. I will give you other books to read – political articles, writings from our own country as well as here. I am standing as the Liberal candidate in a month's time, so it's all hands to the deck . . .

Rani   May I ask you a question, Dadabhai?

Dadabhai   I would be most disappointed if you didn't.

Rani   Why do you want to be a Member of Parliament?

Dadabhai   Good question. I believe in English fair play.

I also believe that we have to educate the British electorate as to the real conditions of India as a preliminary to awakening our call for reform.

Rani   And you can't do that from the outside?

Dadabhai   I have my supporters but not the power to change anything. This British Empire is growing. The Queen is acquiring more and more lands, like a greedy whale, she is swallowing entire countries. Nations are being enslaved. Through taxes, through restrictions on trade, through the looting of our precious minerals.

Rani   So much for English fair play.

Dadabhai   One last thing I need to check, my child. You can write?

Rani   Tolerably.

Dadabhai *thrusts a notepad at* **Rani**.

Dadabhai   Write down what I say. As fast and as legibly as you can. I invite Rani . . . surname?

Rani   Das.

Dadabhai   I invite Rani Das and her child to stay with my family, here in our home for one month to see how she progresses as an assistant. If after that month neither of the parties are happy with the arrangement the contract will be terminated.

Rani *writes fast.*

Dadabhai *takes the piece of paper from* **Rani** *and looks at it.*

Dadabhai   Slightly spidery writing, but it will improve.

You had better not disappoint me, Rani. It would do my reputation no good to have to dismiss a widow and her child after a month.

Rani   I won't disappoint you, Dada. Thank you!

She stands up, excited. She flings her arms suddenly around **Dadabhai***'s neck and then rushes out.* **Dadabhai** *looks perplexed but pleased.*

Dadabhai   Don't forget to come back, my child!

Scene Six

Sally *is sweeping her front yard. A turban-headed Indian man approaches.* **Sally** *looks up.*

Sally   I'm sorry to say, we're packed to the rafters tonight.

Singh   Jai Singh at your service, madam. I am looking for Lascar Sally.

Sally *smiles at* **Singh**.

Sally   You're looking at her. I dare say I could squeeze you in.

Singh   I am not in need of accommodation, thank you. I have come to deliver some letters.

He produces a parcel.

From Hari Sharma.

Sally *takes the letters and looks surprised.*

Sally   So many?

Singh   And this letter is for you.

Sally *takes one more letter.*

Sally   Thank you.

She opens the letter addressed to her. She reads out loud.

Sally   'Dear Sally,' – Hang on! – 'if you come across Rani Das, please pass my letters on to her.

I don't know where she is but I pray you know her. I trust you are in good health, my friend. One day soon, I will return and we will laugh together again. With warmest regards – Hari.' Come on!

Singh   Jai Singh.

Sally *looks at the bundle of letters. We see her taking the letters, walking and handing them over to* **Firoza**. **Firoza** *walks across to* **Rani** *and hands the letters to her. She hugs* **Rani** *as she does so.*

Rani *sits and starts to read the letters.*

Scene Seven

London, 1892.

We are in a drawing room, Indian in decor. Dawn is rising and
Firoza *is dozing in a chair.* **Rani** *is still reading* **Hari***'s letters as
she hears the cheers of a crowd. She quickly puts the letters away
as a group of Indian and English men and women follow her in.
They are in high spirits as they carry* **Dadabhai** *in.* **Rani** *looks
startled at first but is pleased.*

Dadabhai (*laughing*)   For goodness' sake, put me down!

I'm going to fall, you are all too intoxicated . . . Rani, do tell them
to put me down.

William   The new Member of Parliament for the constituency of
Finsbury!

Gandhi   The British electorate have finally kicked Salisbury in
the guts and elected a 'black man'.

The men all carefully place **Dadabhai** *on the ground.* **Rani** *helps
him to a chair.*

Dadabhai   What time is it?

Rani   It is five in the morning, Dada.

Dadabhai   I am quite overcome with the emotion of the night.

William   So you should be. Your constituents were jubilant at
your victory tonight.

Gandhi   You could hear the cheering at St Paul's at one side and
Chelsea Hospital on the other.

Dadabhai   I only just won – very slim margin. A majority of five
over the Tory candidate. There is much work to be done.

William   Our Dadabhai is the first Indian man to represent his
country in Parliament. The very first! The tide is turning.

Rani *picks up a small bundle of papers.*

Rani   Telegrams have been arriving through the night.

She hands them over to **Dadabhai** *who looks through them.*

Dadabhai   'Congratulations from Keir Hardie. See you in the Commons.' Excellent, he won the seat for Westham South . . . 'Finally we have you. John Bright . . .' 'The journey has just begun, my friend. My congratulations, Dada. Ramsay MacDonald.' 'Rejoice beyond measure that you have been elected Liberal MP for Central Finsbury. Florence Nightingale.'

William   This is the advantage of supporting women's suffrage, Dada. You have more lady supporters than any MP I know.

Everyone laughs. **Dadabhai** *continues to smile and peruse the telegrams.*

Dadabhai   Please, sit close to me, Rani, MK, get Rani some cordial. You see? One month here and already I am completely dependent on this little girl.

William   How did you manage without her before, Dada?

Gandhi *gets busy pouring some drinks.* **Rani** *sits down.*

Dadabhai   My friends, we are victorious!

The newspapers are delivered and everyone falls on them.

Dadabhai   I want to hear it all. Do not spare me from the criticism.

Gandhi   Sir Lepel Griffin, one-time chief secretary in the Punjab, speaks out against you.

Dadabhai   As expected. Go on.

Gandhi   'Naoroji is an alien in race, in custom, in religion; destitute of local sympathy or local knowledge, no more unsuitable representative could be imagined or suggested. As to the people of India, Mr Naoroji no more represents them than a Polish Jew settled in Whitechapel represents the people of England. He is a Parsi, a member of a small foreign colony, probably Semitic in origin. The Parsis are the Jews of India; intelligent, industrious and wealthy . . . But they are quite as much aliens to the people of India as the English rulers can possibly be.'

Silence falls in the room.

Dadabhai   At least he concedes we are intelligent and industrious.

William   If you are a 'Jew' of India, what does he suppose Benjamin Disraeli was?

Rani   A Parsi.

Everyone falls about laughing.

Rani   I have a nice one here.

Dadabhai   Read it out, nice and loud so we can all . . .

Rani   Dada . . .

Dadabhai   We are all friends here.

Rani *looks around the room, afraid.*

William   Go on Rani.

Rani (*she reads fluently*)   'In India there are 250 millions of people and it is a monstrous doctrine that until now they have not as much as one representative in the House of Commons. The right policy is to strengthen Parliament by admission of men who know something of the pressing wants of people who were advanced in civilization when Europe was plunged in darkness. Men like Naoroji should be in Parliament because it is desirable that a reliable, well-informed and strong man should speak for the reformers of India with authority. He is after all a trusted representative of the great Indian National Congress.'

Dadabhai   Thank you, Rani.

Dadabhai *and* **Rani** *share a smile.*

Gandhi   Now that you are elected, Dadabhai, will you use your position to fight against the British rule in India?

Dadabhai   My first duty is to my constituency. I intend to support the Liberal Party's programme in Parliament – Irish Home Rule, municipal reform, Women's franchise . . .

Gandhi *looks disappointed.*

Dadabhai   But I will be using my position to raise the level of debate in the Commons about the neglect of our mother country. You will all need to help me. It is time to prove Salisbury and his party that Indians are not inferior, that we have intellect and a democratic sentiment. I believe that English justice and fair play will be triumphant.

Everyone cheers.

Song: 'A promise made'

> A promise made,
> All the nights and days.
> A moment's grace,
> Home is in your embrace,
> *Shagorer on tore bidoy Nilo*
> (Ocean of hearts, cast away)*

Scene Eight

Osborne House, 1897.

During this scene, **Hari** *is digging in a diamond mine.*

Lady Sarah *approaches* **Victoria** *who is writing at her desk in the gardens.*

Lady Sarah   The Prince of Wales asked me to speak with you. It is this trip, ma'am. To Nice.

Victoria   Yes. We are looking forward to it.

* Lyrics by Dom Coyote

Lady Sarah   The Prince of Wales asked me to inform you that the gentlemen of the royal household have refused to go if your Munshi is attending.

Victoria   I beg your pardon?

Lady Sarah   Simply this. If he goes they won't.

Victoria   That is intolerable.

Lady Sarah   His Royal Highness asked me to remind you that the Munshi is a servant, a teacher, but he is not the equal of us and yet you treat him as if he were one of those deposed Indian princes.

Victoria   This is your doing, Lady Sarah?

Lady Sarah   No, ma'am. I am simply conveying the views of your son.

Victoria *is furious.*

Victoria   Abdul will attend with us. He will travel as part of the royal household.

Lady Sarah   They are refusing to come.

Victoria *stands and sweeps all her writing things off her desk in a fury.*

Victoria   Then they are racially prejudiced and jealous of my affection for my Munshi!

Lady Sarah *is rather taken aback.*

Victoria   Nobody, whether family, government or household is ever going to tell me whom I can employ or even have as a friend and confidant. To me, it is a person's character that is important, not their position in the social hierarchy. I refuse to place my trust exclusively in aristocrats and courtiers. I will defend those in whom I place my trust to the last breath in my body.

Lady Sarah   Ma'am.

Victoria   Convey this back to Bertie. Unless the royal court starts to treat our loyal servant with more respect, we will refuse to attend a single event connected to our Diamond Jubilee. Do we make ourselves clear?

Lady Sarah   Perfectly.

She remains standing.

Victoria   You may leave. We have correspondence to write.

Lady Sarah   Ma'am, I have one more message from your son.

Victoria   Why doesn't he tell me himself? What is wrong with Bertie?

Lady Sarah   He fears that Your Majesty does not heed his advice, that you are too blinkered to see what others see. His Highness's words, ma'am, not mine. They will not allow you to make Mr Karim a Companion of the Order of the British Empire.

Victoria   Who are they?

Lady Sarah   Prince Edward, Lord Salisbury and his cabinet.

Victoria   Tell them to just accept the decision and please stop quarrelling with me.

Lady Sarah   Their reasoning is that if you show such favour to a Muslim, then the Hindus will feel betrayed.

Victoria   This is just an excuse. They have all hated Abdul from the moment he stepped into my presence. They want to keep him in place.

A lowly, illiterate Muslim clerk. They will not accept that he is their equal.

Lady Sarah   They are most insistent that you retract the offer.

Victoria   I refuse to. And right now I have rather pressing business on my mind. The Boers have created a frightful situation in Southern Africa. Hundreds of my troops may die on the battlefield and you are beginning to fray my nerves with your constant carping.

Lady Sarah *stands her ground.*

Lady Sarah   I am simply sent as the messenger. His Highness has stated that your attachment to the Munshi is so extreme that the royal household and indeed the government are beginning to question your sanity.

Victoria   My what?

Lady Sarah   Lord Salisbury is in agreement that if you continue to try and make the Munshi a Companion of the British Empire, they will have no alternative but to declare you insane and therefore unfit for office.

Victoria *is silent.*

Lady Sarah   In such a scenario, your son would be crowned King Edward . . . they only wish to protect your reputation, ma'am.

Victoria *stands with difficulty.* **Lady Sarah** *tries to help her, but* **Victoria** *shoos her away. She is upset as she paces and thinks.*

Victoria   My own son would declare me insane and deny me my rights as his mother and Sovereign of this land?

She turns and regards **Lady Sarah**. *She is angry, her voice emotional.*

Victoria   I will write to Bertie and Lord Salisbury myself. Abdul will remain as my Munshi but I will retract the offer of the honour.

Lady Sarah   And Nice?

Victoria   He will attend as my royal servant and not as a member of the royal household.

Lady Sarah *smiles triumphantly and curtseys deeply.* **Victoria** *looks away.*

Scene Nine

Rani *is sitting on a park bench on a sunny day. She is reading the bundle of letters from* **Hari**. *She reads eagerly.* **Firoza** *is sitting by her side.*

Victoria *sits on her own ruminating on her situation.*

Firoza   How many times have you read those letters?

Rani   He writes well. The words get more and more accomplished. He is reading books.

Firoza   You must have inspired him.

Rani   He talks of great hardships. In this one, he spends almost the entire voyage with a fever, in the next one, his friend is clapped in irons and dies from the wounds inflicted by the manacles. Terrible, terrible . . .

Firoza   A sailor's life is not easy and the lascars are treated badly.

Rani   In this one he talks of digging in the diamond mines of Africa. And in the next (*She laughs.*) he is walking in the sun! Listen!

'My dearest Rani,

I write these words to you on land now.

We are docked back in Calcutta and I have been eating sweet, hot jalebi in the sun and walking about the city. It is good to be home but my regret is that I am seeing it on my own without you and so the picture is not right.'

That is the last one dated a year ago.

Firoza   Sally hasn't had any more since then.

Rani   I wonder what became of him?

Firoza   Rani, you're not still hankering after this Hari are you? He's a lascar –, you're an educated young woman now.

When am I going to see you settled down with a nice strong man?

Rani *smiles and looks away.*

Firoza   You could have anyone you want. I see the way some of the men around Dadabhai look at you. William, Gandhi, and now this brilliant young lawyer, what's his name?

Rani   Muhammad Ali Jinnah?

Firoza   Exactly!

Rani   Firoza!

Firoza   It's true. But you only want to serve Dadabhai and read those old letters.

Rani   What about you, Firoza? You never remarried?

Firoza   I don't like men so much. Don't trust them.

Rani (*laughs*)   And you're trying to persuade me to find a man! It's funny to think that when I arrived, I just wanted to meet the Queen.

Firoza   What for? To thank her for having ruined India for two or three generations to come? There is talk about another famine in India. It is pitiful.

Rani   The British are doing nothing to prevent it.

Do you think Hari is still alive?

Firoza *looks at* **Rani**.

Firoza   Rani, I don't know. Sally has heard nothing.

No one has heard from Hari for a long time.

Rani *looks upset. She takes* **Rani**'s *hand*.

Rani   I have Asha, I have you, my dear Firoza, and I have Dadabhai.

Abdul *enters*.

Victoria   Oh Abdul. I'm so sorry.

Scene Ten

1897 – year of the Queen's Diamond Jubilee.

Kipling's poem 'The White Man's Burden' *is set to music and sung:*

Take up the White Man's burden –
Send forth the best ye breed –

Go bind your sons to exile
To serve your captives' need;
To wait in heavy harness,
On fluttered folk and wild –
Your new-caught, sullen peoples,
Half-devil and half-child.

Take up the White Man's burden –
In patience to abide,
To veil the threat of terror
And check the show of pride;
By open speech and simple,
An hundred times made plain
To seek another's profit,
And work another's gain . . .

*In the backdrop we see archive photos/film of the Queen's
procession through the streets.*

NB: During this scene we see **Hari***, now dressed in a basic suit
with shoes on his feet, stepping off a boat.*

There is a moment here when **Rani** *sees* **Victoria** *in the Jubilee
procession.*

Scene Eleven

1897.

We split the scene between **Victoria** *being dressed for her
Diamond Jubilee dinner and* **Dadabhai***'s speech.*

Victoria *is being dressed, with diamonds strung round her neck
and in her cap.*

We cut to:

Dadabhai *is standing in Parliament making a speech.* **Rani** *is
there listening to him.*

Dadabhai   The foreign invaders of former times in India
returned to their country laden with spoils and there was an end

to the evil. India by her industry soon made up the gap in her national wealth.

But entirely different has the past India received blows and bruises here and there, but her vital blood was not lost. Now, as the country is being continually bled, its vitality and vigour is low.

We cut to: **Victoria** *as she is adorned with jewels, etc.* **Abdul** *enters.*

Abdul   Ma'am, we are ready for you. You look splendid.

Victoria   Do you like the gold detail? It was especially embroidered for me in India.

Abdul   Absolutely gorgeous, ma'am.

Victoria   Who is here?

Abdul   Everyone. Foreign royalties, special ambassadors and envoys, the family. And they are all waiting for you in the supper room . . . little tables of twelve each.

Cut back to **Dadabhai**'s *speech.*

Dadabhai   Even as we stand here, waving our flags and wishing Her Majesty well, in India, famine has swept over much of the north and west, followed by a major plague epidemic. These tragedies are compounded by the Raj's apathetic response to the famine and its imposition of draconian plague regulations.

Cut to **Victoria**.

Victoria   You know I touched an electric button this morning. Apparently it started a message which was telegraphed right across my Empire. 'From my heart I thank my beloved people. May God bless them!' And the sun burst out.

She stands. Her ladies-in-waiting stand back in admiration and curtsey to her.

Abdul   Do you not want the wheelchair, ma'am?

Victoria   I prefer to walk. Just give me your arm.

She takes **Abdul**'s *arm.*

Abdul   So much affection from your subjects. You must be very proud today.

Victoria   No, Abdul, not proud but – humble.

Cut to: **Dadabhai**'s *speech.*

Dadabhai   Millions of Indian men, women and children are dying. Millions more will die unless financial resources are directed back to the people.

So I say to you all, the Diamond Jubilee should be celebrated in a manner befitting a monarch who has been 'the Empress of Famine and the Queen of Black Death'. I accuse the British of inflicting upon Indians 'all the scourges of the world – war, pestilence and famine'.

As **Victoria** *is led from the room by* **Abdul***, we hear a band start up.*

Voices   Three cheers for the Queen!

Hip, hip – HOORAY! Hip, hip – HOORAY!

Hip, hip – HOORAY!

There is much cheering as **Victoria** *and* **Abdul** *exit.*

Scene Twelve

1900.

We see **Sally** *standing and sprucing up* **Hari**'s *outfit, suit, etc. She stands back and surveys him, satisfied. Then she pushes* **Hari** *on. They walk together.*

In **Dadabhai**'s *drawing room.* **Dadabhai** *is packing up his room. He is throwing books into a box, gathering papers, etc.* **Rani** *is watching on, distraught.*

Rani   You're giving up!

Dadabhai   I am not. I am going back to live my old age out in my motherland, surrounded by people who listen to me. I believed in British fairness but actually it's a myth. John Bull is nothing more than an opium peddler, a slave trader and a violent thug.

Rani   You are leaving me behind?

Dadabhai   Look at this Boer War – the entire might of the British Empire against a handful of Boer farmers. Burning and looting entire villages . . . the concentration camps . . . it is not worthy of so-called British fairness and justice. This is not war, this is massacre on a grand scale. Monstrous! Gandhi has been sending me correspondence. Apparently he has set up an ambulance corps so that Indians out there can give their services as stretcher bearers. Even Gandhi is working with the corps in the field – carrying the wounded through heavy firing.

Rani   Dadabhai, you are distressed.

Dadabhai   This war-mongering Tory government, the killing, torture – our troops, innocent civilians all done in the name of the Empire. The electorate here only voted Salisbury back in because of their misplaced jingoistic ideas of nationalism. Why should Britain own the whole of South Africa? Why should such a small island rule the world?

Rani   You're really going to leave all your work here behind?

Dadabhai   I spent some years in the Commons making speeches and recommendations. Apart from a handful of friends, they all simply ignored me. I thought that perhaps the British would see the error of their ways, that they would understand how much they have taken from our land whilst our people starve in their millions! But they don't care and this war is further proof of their inhumanity.

Rani *looks distraught.*

Dadabhai   I came to this country in 1855. I have done my time. I want to be in India, to work through the Indian National Congress. To fight the British through peaceful means.

Rani   Dada, if you give up hope, then we will all fail.

Dadabhai   I am not giving up hope, Rani, simply understanding that I have to take a different path. In India I can make a difference.

Self-government is the only remedy for her woes and through India's example the other colonies will take heart and rise against them.

Rani   What about me? How can you leave me and Asha?

Dadabhai *looks at* **Rani** *with affection and holds her hands.*

Rani   I will come with you, Dadabhai.

Dadabhai   No, Rani.

Rani   Why?

Dadabhai   You have your daughter, your friends here.

William says he can find you a position as a teacher in a girls' school.

Rani *is upset.*

Dadabhai   I am an old man now. I want to go home.

You must make your own way in life.

He looks up as **Sally** *and* **Hari** *stands in the doorway.*

Hari   Excuse me, sir . . . sorry to disturb you . . . your secretary showed me in . . . I hope you don't mind but I came to see Rani.

Sally   I found him for you, Rani.

Rani *is glued to the chair as she stares in disbelief at* **Hari**. *He is well dressed in a brown suit and his hair is trim and slicked back.*

Dadabhai *looks from* **Hari** *to* **Rani**.

Dadabhai   And you are?

Hari   My name is Hari.

Dadabhai   Hari!

Hari   We met . . . a long time ago . . . I am an old friend . . . erm acquaintance of Rani's.

Dadabhai   Aaahh . . . yes, yes, of course. Come in.

Rani *is still unable to speak.* **Dadabhai** *looks at a bit of loss as to know what to do.*

Sally *nudges* **Hari** *to talk.*

Sally   Go on!

Hari   Rani, although I don't think I can ever be your . . . I have started up a small business . . . I did not return the rich man I wanted to be for your sake . . . but I make furniture in Whitechapel . . . and have a little money saved . . . I rent a set of small rooms above the business and . . . I thought . . . before it was too late . . . I should like to be your friend again . . .

Sally   Rani, if you won't have him, I will.

Dadabhai   Come, Sally. Let's leave these two alone.

Rani, just call me if you need me.

Dadabhai *tries to leave but* **Rani** *clings to him, afraid.*

Dadabhai   I will be in the next room Rani.

He looks at **Rani***.*

Dadabhai   Come now. Have courage, my child.

Rani *lets go of* **Dadabhai** *and he exits, patting* **Hari** *affectionately as he leaves and shoving him gently further into the room.* **Sally** *looks at* **Hari** *meaningfully before leaving the room.* **Rani** *is highly emotional.*

Hari   Rani.

Rani *backs away and collapses in a chair.*

Rani   You look well, Hari.

Hari   You've blossomed into a woman, little Rani.

Rani   I am not your little Rani anymore. How long have you been in England?

Hari   Three years.

Rani   Three years!

Hari   I wanted to come before but. . .I had nothing to offer.

Rani   I am settled now. I have friends and work and I have a daughter.

Hari   I heard. You are blessed.

He steps closer. **Rani** *turns away from him.*

Rani   You abandoned me.

Hari   It was not easy for me to find you. You were the one that disappeared.

Rani   You should have looked harder for me.

Hari   Sally said she delivered my letters to you.

Rani   I read them.

They were beautiful.

Hari *weeps.* **Rani** *is moved. She steps closer to* **Hari**.

Rani   I am so sorry for your suffering. But I wish you had come back sooner.

Thirteen years have passed Hari.

Hari   Is there anyone?

Rani   No.

For you?

Hari   No one that ever came close to how I felt for you.

Rani   I still don't understand why you stopped writing?

Hari   I didn't want to hold you back. Hold you to a promise that we made in another time. After all, I was just a sailor, a lascar.

Rani   I was just an ayah.

Hari   But now, you are an educated, accomplished, clever woman. What would you want with a brute like me?

Rani *remains silent.* **Hari** *watches her carefully.*

Hari   I am glad I saw you again. Perhaps in time we can be friends again but maybe too many years have passed and we have missed our moment.

He looks entreatingly at **Rani** *but she does not respond.*

Hari   I will take my leave of you. Please give my fondest regards to Dadabhai.

He turns to leave. **Rani** *stands up on shaky legs.*

Rani   Hari – don't go!

She almost falls and **Hari** *rushes forward to hold her up. They embrace, kiss and cry.*

Rani   I missed you so much. I was so young . . . I didn't understand my own feelings . . .

Hari   Every night I thought of your happy, smiling face. Seeing you again has made me feel like a sailor feels when he has been drifting on an endless swell of sea and then he spots the land. The relief! The joy! Knowing that he will stand on firm ground.

Tell me you still feel something for me?

Rani

'I closed my lids, and kept them close,
And the balls like pulses beat;
For the sky and the sea, and the sea and the sky
Lay like a load on my weary eye, And the dead were at my feet.'

Hari   I am so pleased you have made such a good life for yourself. I knew you could. But from now, I want to be there with you.

Rani   Don't ever leave me again.

Hari Never.

Rani Never.

They kiss passionately.

Scene Thirteen

1900.

Victoria *is reclined in a chaise longue. She looks unwell but is supported by cushions and pillows, etc.*

Abdul *enters.*

He plumps up the pillows for **Victoria**.

Victoria Apparently we now have conquered Benin and the lands of south-west Nigeria are part of our Empire. Our consul was ambushed and sadly massacred. The people of Benin are now liberated.

Abdul, I feel too unwell today to take my lessons.

Abdul Has Doctor Reid given you some draughts?

Victoria *nods.*

Victoria Last night I dreamt of my dear Ponsonby. I do miss him. He was so universally beloved – so just and fair. To have been snatched away so suddenly . . .

Abdul We are all mortal, ma'am. Death comes to everyone.

Victoria It is hard for those who are left behind.

I wish people didn't have to die.

Abdul There is a story in our Koran about a rich businessman who called the Angel of Death to him and asked him for a favour. He said, would you please give me warning before I am about to die, just so that I can prepare myself? The Angel of Death agreed and said he would send a sign. Then one day, when the businessman was counting his money, he was visited by that same Angel. The businessman cried out 'No! I am not ready! You promised me you would give me a sign before you came. I received no sign!' The Angel replied, 'Allah gave you many signs. Has your hair not turned grey? Your skin wrinkled? Your eyesight poor? Have you not become an old man? These were all signs but you refused to heed them.' And so the rich businessman had no choice but to go with the Angel of Death. When it is our time, nothing can prevent it.

Victoria *is quiet for some time.*

Abdul   Ma'am, I have a small surprise for you.

Victoria   I am too exhausted for surprises.

Abdul   You don't have to do anything, ma'am, you simply have to watch and let it all flow over you.

Victoria   What mischief are you up to, Abdul?

Abdul   You have always said how much you wished you could go to India?

Victoria   It is too late now. I can barely stand. Perhaps next summer, if I am up to it . . . I would have liked to have visited the Taj Mahal and sat by the Ganges in the moonlight, I would have liked to have ridden on an elephant!

Abdul   I have taken the liberty, Your Majesty, to ensure that if Her Majesty can't go to India, then we will bring India to her.

Victoria *looks bemused.* **Abdul** *smiles, claps his hands and a troupe of brightly coloured musicians and performers enter.*

Victoria   Abdul!

Abdul *stands nearby, half-leaning against* **Victoria**. *Together they start to watch the performance.* **Victoria** *looks delighted.*

At the end, **Victoria** *claps her hands. When the troupe have exited,* **Victoria** *looks up at* **Abdul** *in gratitude and love.*

Scene Fourteen

Osborne House, 22 January 1901.

Lights up on an ornate white open coffin in which **Victoria** *lies. The royal household all walk up to the coffin one by one, including Indian servants. It is a sombre occasion.* **Lady Sarah** *stands. A young* **Page** *approaches* **Lady Sarah**.

Page   Excuse me, Lady Sarah.

Lady Sarah   What is it?

Page   The Munshi wishes to say his final farewells.

Lady Sarah *looks very irritated.*

Lady Sarah   Very well. Send him in.

The **Page** *exits and re-enters with* **Abdul**. **Abdul** *bows deeply to* **Lady Sarah** *who simply nods her head.* **Abdul** *carries a single white rose, which he places carefully on* **Victoria**'s *person.* **Lady Sarah** *looks away as* **Abdul** *weeps silently over the coffin. Two undertakers step forward and nail the coffin down.* **Abdul** *steps back. He looks shaken.*

Lady Sarah *approaches* **Abdul**.

Lady Sarah   Mr Karim. I have instructions from the King. He wishes you to gather all correspondence from Her Majesty to you and you are to remain under escort until such time that we have ascertained that all letters have been collected. Under supervision by the Master of the House and witnessed by myself, the letters will be burned. You will then gather your belongings, your family and others related to you now living in the royal grounds and you will return to India. His Majesty says that he has no further use for your services. Have I made myself clear, Mr Karim?

Abdul   Yes, Lady Sarah.

Lady Sarah   You will return to your home under royal escort and be allowed to retain your house in Agra. However, as soon as you have returned, we will be obliged to search your house for further correspondence to you from Her Majesty and other small mementoes. These too will be reclaimed or destroyed. Do I have your full co-operation on this matter?

Abdul   Yes, Lady Sarah.

Lady Sarah *turns, bows one last time to the coffin and moves to exit the room.*

Lady Sarah   Seal the room when it has been cleared.

Pages *enter, with letters and transcripts. One by one they strip* **Abdul** *of his royal livery, his turban, jacket, etc. They re-dress him as an ordinary civilian. As the letters pile up around him we hear the sound of a huge crackling bonfire which intensifies and fills the stage with a red glow.*

All of the Munshi's letters from Queen Victoria are burned.

Scene Fifteen

1901.

We are back at Tilbury docks. It is full of people saying their fond farewells. **Rani** *and* **Hari** *have come to see* **Dadabhai** *off.* **Rani** *is wearing a red bridal sari.*

Abdul *walks proudly at the back flanked on either side by English officials.*

Dadabhai, **Hari** *and* **Rani** *clock them.*

Dadabhai *shakes hands with* **Hari**.

Dadabhai   Look after yourself, Hari. You're a family man now.

Hari   I'm a very lucky man. I won't say 'goodbye' because I know we will meet again.

Rani *hugs* **Dadabhai** *suddenly. He is choked.*

Dadabhai   I've said a lot of farewells in my time, Rani.

But you break my heart. I must go . . . and God bless you.

Rani *waves as* **Dadabhai** *exits to go up to the boat.* **Dadabhai**
waves back and exits.

Hari   Are you alright?

Rani *nods, slightly tearful.*

Hari   Now it's just us, Rani. We're going to make a good life
together here with Asha. I will always be here by your side.

Rani *hugs* **Hari**.

She turns and watches as **Abdul** *is kneeling on the ground
by the gang plank. He is kissing the ground.*

Hari   Isn't that the viceroy's man?

Rani *and* **Hari** *approach* **Abdul**.

Hari   Excuse me, brother.

Abdul *turns and looks at* **Hari** *and then* **Rani**. *They both do
namaste to* **Abdul**.

Abdul   We have met before?

Rani   Briefly.

Abdul   I can't quite . . .?

Rani   1887, when I first came here, you were on the same boat.

Abdul   Fourteen years ago. I remember now. The young ayah.
Abdul Karim at your service.

Abdul *does adaab to both* **Rani** *and* **Hari**.

Rani   Rani Das, I mean Rani Sharma, at yours.

Hari *smiles at* **Rani**.

Hari   Hari Sharma. Please, excuse me.

He retreats to talk to the serang.

Abdul   Is that the rascal lascar that was following you around
everywhere? He looks very smart.

Rani   It is. You see? I took your advice. I've chosen my friends very carefully. Are you sad to be leaving?

Abdul   It will be good to see my home again. This is a strange, intoxicating island.

Rani   Yes! At once magical but at the same time unforgiving.

Abdul   Unforgiving – yes.

Rani   Is it true that you worked for the royal house?

Abdul   Yes.

Rani   And you met the Queen?

Abdul   Yes. I served her.

Rani   What was she like?

Abdul   She was a great woman. So different from the people that surrounded her – the family, court officials, the ladies-in-waiting. She had a curiosity which was boundless.

Rani   She had a lot of power.

Abdul   So much power in her hands. The lands she ruled gravitated around her, like planets circling the sun. But she never ventured out. You and I have travelled further in our short lives than she ever did. All she had were her imaginings.

And what about you? Are you still an ayah? You don't look like one anymore.

Rani   I was educated. Now I am a teacher and I am hoping to set up a school.

Abdul   We are both teachers then.

Rani   Will you be going back to teach?

Abdul   No. I don't think so. I will have to find some other occupation.

Rani   Didn't you enjoy teaching?

Abdul   It wasn't that – just that once you have had the ultimate student, where else can you go?

Rani (*realizing*)   You are the Queen's Munshi?

Abdul   Was. I have nothing to remember her by.

They ordered me to return everything else you see.

Rani   But you have your memories.

Do you remember you gave me something when my master and mistress had abandoned me?

Abdul   My father's compass.

Rani *produces the compass.* **Abdul** *looks at it carefully.*

She tries to press it into **Abdul***'s hand.*

Abdul   No, please, it was a gift.

Rani   Take it. Perhaps it too will bring you luck.

Abdul   May Allah be with you.

He takes the compass and does adaab. The royal guards surround **Abdul** *and he exits towards the boat.*

Hari *steps forward and puts his arm around* **Rani***.*

Lights fade as **Rani** *and* **Hari** *laugh together.*

The End.

Notes

Page 5

Lascar: Originally (from the seventeenth century) a term applying just to Indian sailors, it came to be applied to all non-European sailors, including men of Chinese, Arab and East African origin. The majority, however, continued to come from Gujurat and Malabar. By 1914, lascars represented 17.5 per cent of the sailors on British registered ships. They were paid less than European sailors, and had worse conditions of labour. Once steamships became dominant, they were especially recruited to stoke boilers, on the mistaken assumption that their background would make them better at withstanding extreme heat. Whilst they were supposed only to be discharged in India, many jumped ship and settled in Britain, especially in the port cities of London, Liverpool, Glasgow and Cardiff.

Clan Line: A shipping line which originated in a company set up in Liverpool in 1877 to serve the route to Bombay/Mumbai. It became the Clan Line in 1881 following a merger with a Scottish firm, and through various further expansions extended its routes to South Africa, the Persian Gulf and North America. Like other merchant navy shipping lines, it had a repertoire of parodic popular songs, often obscene, which were sung in a mixture of English and seamen's Hindustani, and made fun of officers and stewards.

Blighty: A slang term for England, popular from the 1890s, and especially during the First World War, it derives from the Bengali word *bileti*, meaning 'foreign', which had been used in India to refer to the British throughout the nineteenth century. A popular First World War song was 'There's a ship that's bound for Blighty'.

Listing to port: When a ship is tilting to the left.

Bum engineers: Useless engineers.

Tindal: From the Mayalam 'tantal', an Indian term for a petty officer – second bosun/boatswain – in charge of lascars.

Kasab: A lamp-trimmer.

'Sparkies': Radio officers.

Purser: Steward, always regarded in sailors' songs as potentially gay ('limp-wristed').

'Kala Pani': Black water – that is, the open sea.

Page 6

Jewel in the Crown: The Indian subcontinent was regarded as Britain's imperial 'Jewel in the Crown' – that is, its most valuable possession.

Ayah: An Anglo-Indian term (originally from the Portuguese *aia*) for a nursemaid or nanny employed by European families in India or other parts of the Empire to look after children on sea voyages to and from Britain and on other routes around the Empire.

Page 7

Serang: Bosun/boatswain/petty officer on a ship.

Page 8

Scots Navy: Another term for the Clan Line.

Hooghli run: The Hooghli is a 260-km-long distributary of the River Ganges which flows into the Bay of Bengal. Like the rest of the Ganges, it is considered sacred by Hindus. It is a tidal river, and the major port of Calcutta/Kolkata is on it.

Page 10

Sinbad: Sinbad the sailor is the hero of one of the tales in the *Arabian Nights*, also known as *The Thousand and One Nights*. These ancient tales were supposed to have been told every night by Scheherazade, the wife of the Sultan, to save herself from execution. Sinbad was a rich citizen of Baghdad who went on seven voyages, making fabulous discoveries –

including the giant egg of a huge white bird, the roc, which carries him to a remote valley, the bed of which is strewn with diamonds. Merchants have discovered that fatty meat thrown in sticks to the diamonds, which eagles then carry out and take to their nests, from which the merchants retrieve them. Sinbad himself escapes by attaching himself to a piece of meat, and is rescued by a merchant. He goes back to Baghdad with a sackful of diamonds. The legend of the diamonds is told in many variations from the stories told by Alexander the Great's soldiers on their return from India in the fourth century BCE. Although this reference in the play can be heard as a more casual reference to a famous sailor, the associations with India (and Ceylon/Sri Lanka, which was an island of jewels) and with diamonds (mines to be exploited by adventuring capitalists, as well as the Queen Empress's Diamond Jubilee) give a more complex resonance.

Page 11

Shukria: Thank you.

Page 12

Lackee: servant

Dadabhai Naoroji: Dadabhai Naoroji (1825–1917) was an Indian merchant, politician and writer, who was elected MP for Finsbury Central in 1892 (until 1895), and co-founded the Indian National Congress in 1885, of which he was three times elected president (1886, 1893 and 1906).

Gandhi: Mohandas Karamchand Ghandi (1869–1948) was an Indian lawyer who developed a campaign of non-violence to press for Indian independence. The name Mahatma, meaning 'venerable', was first applied to him in South Africa in 1914, but came into universal use. He became leader of the Indian National Congress in 1921. He mobilized across India in support of the rights of lower-caste people, untouchables and women, and promoted the merits of religious pluralism and communal unity. He was assassinated on 30 January 1948 by a young Hindu who held him responsible for Partition.

East India Association: Founded in London in 1866 by Dadabhai Naoroji (together with other Indians and retired British officials) as a pressure group for discussing and promoting Indian issues. It had 600 members by

1868 and 1000 in 1878. It produced a journal which published the lectures given at its meetings in Caxton Hall, Westminster.

Lord Salisbury: Conservative Prime Minister of the United Kingdom, 1885–86, 1886–92 and 1895–1902.

Page 13

namaste: A Sanskrit term (found in Hindu sacred texts and enacted in early temple statues) for a respectful or reverential greeting.

Page 15

'Water, water, everywhere . . .': Rani is reading from Samuel Taylor Coleridge's poem *The Rime of the Ancient Mariner* (first published in 1798). A sailor coming back from a long voyage stops a man on his way in to a wedding party and starts telling his long narrative, which is a poem about storytelling and its place in the interplay between nature, human agency and the supernatural. It creates vivid images of the superstitious world of the sailors and the hallucinatory impact of being long at sea.

Page 19

Tilbury docks: An extension of the London docks, designed for steamships, which was authorized by Act of Parliament in 1882, and finally opened in 1886.

Page 29

Lascar Sally: An Englishwoman called Sarah Graham, who ran a lodging house for seamen in Wapping. Like 'Calcutta Louise', she had an Indian partner and spoke Hindi fluently.

Page 54

aloo gobi: A dish of potatoes, cauliflower and spices.

chicken korma: A chicken stew braised with yoghurt, coconut milk and almonds.

Page 59

Bertie: Albert Edward, the eldest son of Queen Victoria. Born in 1841, he was the Prince of Wales for nearly 60 years, becoming King and Emperor of India in 1901, and reigning as Edward VII until his death in 1910. His relationship with his mother was always strained. In 1875–76 he went on a very successful eight-month tour of India, where he expressed his strong opposition to religious and racial prejudice.

Page 60

Balmoral: An estate in Scotland bought in 1852 by Prince Albert, Queen Victoria's husband. A new castle was completed in 1856. Because they had so much enjoyed being there together, after Albert's death the Queen stayed for more extensive periods. It was during the intense initial period of mourning that she developed a close relationship with John Brown, a ghillie (outdoor servant) on the estate. Controversy over this friendship was the precursor to that over Abdul Karim.

Page 61

Khitmagar: An Indian word for a waiter or butler.

Munshi: Originally a Persian word, used in the Mughal Empire and British India for a teacher, translator or secretary.

Von Angeli: Heinrich von Angeli (1840–1925) was an Austrian artist, who painted many portraits of the Queen and her family.

Page 62

Lascars' song: '*Eki Dumah*': Stan Hugill, in his *Shanties from the Seven Seas* (1961), reports this song being picked up in the West Indies, probably originating with a lascar crew, as the words are a mixture of pidgin English and Hindi.

Page 64

Lord Ponsonby: Henry Frederick Ponsonby (1825–95) served in
the British Army until he became Queen Victoria's Private Secretary
(1870–95). From 1878 he was also Keeper of the Privy Purse. A
consummate diplomat, he worked hard to maintain lines of communication
between the Queen and the Liberal Party, and to prevent her dignity being
undermined by her relationships with John Brown and Abdul Karim.

Page 65

Rafiuddin Ahmed: Sir Raffiudin Ahmed (1865–1954) was an Indian
barrister, politician and journalist, who was a close friend of Abdul Karim,
and was an important member of the Muslim Patriotic League. He was
known as the Moulvi (doctor of Islamic law).

Indian League: Founded in 1875 by Sisir Kumar Ghosh in Calcutta/
Kolkata to foster the campaign for self-government.

Indian Home Rule: Self-government for India, by analogy with Irish
Home Rule.

Page 66

Workhouse: Institutions set up under the New Poor Law of 1834, on the
principle of 'less eligibility' (whereby conditions would be made deliberately
unattractive so as to incentivize work and deter pauperism). Popularly
known as 'bastilles' (after the Bastille in Paris, a royal prison which was
stormed as a symbol of arbitrary power on 14 July 1789), they became
emblematic of what was widely held to be an unfair treatment of the poor.
Although their material structure and operation changed over time, the name
and the image remained, as shorthand for an inhumane system.

Page 68

Lord Lansdowne: Henry Petty-Fitzmaurice, fifth Marquess of
Lansdowne (1845–1927), was Viceroy of India from 1888 to 1894.

Page 70

Ganesh ('built like a god'): Ganesh is the elephant-headed Hindu god of prosperity (hence also of beginnings), and also of wisdom.

Page 74

Home for Ayahs: A hostel for ayahs from the Indian subcontinent, Chinese amahs and other non-European women who looked after children on board ships, either on a one-off or a regular basis. In 1891 it was at 6 Jewry Street, Aldgate in east London, but in 1900, when it was taken over by the London City Mission, it was moved to Mare Street, Hackney (in 1921 it was moved again to a larger building). The original Home for Ayahs may have been founded as early as 1825. The Home was intended to provide shelter and food for displaced ayahs. It also helped to negotiate employment opportunities.

Page 80

Cecil Rhodes: Cecil Rhodes (1853–1902) was a gold and diamond mining adventurer and entrepreneur in South Africa, who founded Rhodesia (now Zambia and Zimbabwe), which his South Africa Company named after him in 1895. In 1888, he co-founded De Beers Consolidated Mines, of which he became chairman. He served as Prime Minister of the Cape Colony from 1890 to 1896. He used his time in office to push through legislation in support of his racist and imperialist views, expropriating the lands of black Africans and limiting their franchise. He dreamed of a federation of the Anglo-Saxon race from the Cape to Cairo.

Page 82

Uganda – Lugard: Frederick Dealtry Lugard, Baron Lugard of Abinger (1858–1945), was a soldier and administrator who was born in Madras, and served in the army in India, Sudan and Burma. Working for the Imperial British East African Company in the late 1880s, he made his way to Uganda, and was influential in persuading the British government to take it over as a protectorate in 1894.

Page 83

'Slavery has been abolished': The Slave Trade Act of 1807 abolished the international slave trade. The Slavery Abolition Act of 1833 abolished slavery in the British Empire except for the lands in the possession of the East India Company, Ceylon and St Helena. These exceptions were removed in 1843. Undercover slave-trading continued, and slavery remained present in many parts of the world. The British and Foreign Anti-Slavery Society, founded in 1839, continued (and continues) to campaign against slavery on a global basis.

Page 84

'The Heathen at our Gate': This is an imaginative association which conflates the notion of the 'barbarians at the gate' – the Roman Empire's resistance to the Goths (whom they regarded as uncivilized) who wanted to enter Roman territory, and a series of biblical (Old Testament) texts about the wicked at the gates of the righteous (e.g. Proverbs, 14:19).

Page 85

Bengali Baboos: A term of respect applied to English-speaking Bengali clerks, lawyers or administrators.

Vikings: Norse seafarers (from the area of present-day Norway, Sweden and Denmark), who from the eighth to the eleventh centuries undertook widespread sea voyages as far afield as the Middle East and North America. They conducted raids on and plundered large parts of Europe, also settling in some areas, such as northern and eastern England.

Charles Dickens, Thackeray, Jane Austen, the Brontës, Kipling: All were popular nineteenth-century novelists. To end the list with Kipling was strategic, as Rudyard Kipling (1865–1936) was a novelist, poet, short-story writer and essayist who was born in Bombay/Mumbai, and whose imaginative life was framed by India. At the age of five, he and his three-year-old sister were sent to England to stay in a boarding house in Southsea, where they stayed for six years, an experience which Kipling was later to recall with horror, but to connect to his development as a writer: 'it made me give attention to the lies I soon found it necessary to tell: and this, I presume, is the foundation of literary effort'. He returned to live in Lahore from 1882 to 1887, where he was influenced by both Freemasonry and Buddhism. Kipling's work has been subject to waves of interpretation and reinterpretation in relation to his views on empire.

Page 88

St Paul's: St Paul's Cathedral, London, was built to designs by Christopher Wren, after the destruction of the old cathedral in the Great Fire of London of 1666. On 22 June 1897, a thanksgiving service was held at the foot of the west steps in celebration of Queen Victoria's Diamond Jubilee. After it, the Queen made a six-mile procession round London, where 25,000 seats had been erected along the route.

Chelsea Hospital: The Royal Hospital, Chelsea, was also designed by Christopher Wren, in response to a decree by King Charles II in 1681 to build a home for old soldiers. It was finished in 1692, and by March of that year there were 476 pensioners – the full number. It is still serving its original purpose.

Page 89

Keir Hardie: Keir Hardie (1856–1915) was a Scottish miner and trade unionist, who was an independent MP for West Ham (in the east end of London) from 1892 to 1895. In 1893 he co-founded the Independent Labour Party (ILP). Having lost his seat in West Ham, he was elected to Merthyr Tydfil in 1900, remaining MP until 1915. In 1900 he was involved in the formation of the Labour Representation Committee (LRC), which became the Labour Party, of which he was the first parliamentary leader from 1906 to 1908.

John Bright: John Bright (1811–89) was a Lancashire Radical Liberal, who was a famous orator and campaigned tirelessly for free trade. He was MP successively for Durham (1843), Manchester (1847) and Birmingham (1857–1889).

Ramsay MacDonald: With Keir Hardie and Arthur Henderson, James Ramsay MacDonald (1866–1937) was one of the co-founders of the LRC/ Labour Party, of which he became leader in 1922. He was to become the first Labour Prime Minister in 1924, and then again from 1929 to 1931. From 1931 to 1935 he headed a National Government in which the Conservatives dominated.

Florence Nightingale: Florence Nightingale (1820–1910) became famous as a nursing supervisor during the Crimean War (1853–56), becoming known as 'The Lady with the Lamp'. She established a nursing school in London, and pioneered hospital planning.

Sir Lepel Griffin: Sir Lepel Henry Griffin (1838–1908) was an administrator of British India, starting his career in 1860 in Lahore, and in 1880 becoming Chief Secretary of the Punjab. He was sent on a special mission to Afghanistan, and subsequently appointed Governor-General's Agent in Central India, and Resident in Indore and Hyderabad (although he never actually took up this last post, disappointed not to be made Lieutenant-Governor of the Punjab). A flamboyant character, modelled on the Romantic poet Byron, he was never regarded as wholly reliable. He thought of himself as a friend to Indians, but had a very conservative and abstract view of what this might mean, and was very hostile to cultural miscegenation (as the comments cited in the play indicate). He chaired the East India Association on his return to Britain.

'Polish Jew in Whitechapel': Whitechapel had the densest immigrant population in east London. Poor Jews arrived in 1884 following persecution in Russia. The Poles were expelled from Prussia in 1886. In 1891–92 large numbers were expelled from Moscow and Kiev, and there was further migration following pogroms in Russia in the first years of the twentieth century. The Jews brought with them a religious and welfare-based associational culture, forming *khevres* (societies) which were named after the places from which they had come. Their separateness in customs and language led to moral panics about political subversion. Rising concerns about alien sedition also led to rhetorical overlays of different forms of xenophobia: Jews were accused of pretending to be Muslims in order to foster instability.

Parsis . . . Jews of India: Parsis emigrated to India from Persia in the early middle ages. Zoroastrian in religion, and increasingly focused on the benefits of education, they were regarded from the seventeenth century by

East India Company officials as skilful and conscientious, a reputation that persisted into the nineteenth century. Late-nineteenth-century anti-Semitism combined anxieties about Jewish cleverness and hard work (and greed, leading to economic success) with concerns about the Jews as agents of pauperization and degeneration. Hence the Aliens Act of 1905, the first formal piece of legislation restricting immigration, was focused on keeping out the lowest class of Jewish East European immigrants (South Asian sailors, whilst part of the British Empire, were already restricted by the nature of their employment contracts).

Page 90

Benjamin Disraeli: Benjamin Disraeli (1804–81) was a Conservative politician and novelist who served twice as prime minister (in 1868 and 1874–80). In 1876 he was made Earl of Beaconsfield. He was a particular favourite of the Queen. Jewish by birth, he was baptized into the Anglican Church in 1817. He continued to take pride in his Jewishness and to emphasize the contribution of the Jews to English history.

Indian National Congress: Founded in Bombay/Mumbai in 1885 to promote the cause of Indian independence. Its first General Secretary was a retired British member of the Indian Civil Service, Allan Hume, who got permission from the Viceroy to found an Indian National Union, and in October 1885 he and a group of Indians published 'An Appeal to the Electors of Great Britain and Ireland' to support candidates in the general election of that year who supported Indian concerns. Its failure led to the formation of the Indian National Congress in December, with Womesh Chunder Bonnerjee as President. Most of the founders were from Bombay and Madras provinces; in addition, there were two other British men.

Page 91

Irish Home Rule: The constitutional campaign for Irish self-government, which started with attempts to repeal the Act of Union (of 1801) in the 1840s, but became known as the Home Rule movement in the 1870s. In 1870 Isaac Butt founded the Irish Home Government Association, which became the Home Rule League in 1874. The Government of Ireland Act of 1914, which implemented the 3rd Home Rule Bill, was immediately suspended for the duration of the war, by the end of which circumstances had significantly changed. The Government of Ireland Act of 1920 partitioned Ireland, setting up two Home Rule parliaments, and in 1922 the Anglo-Irish Treaty following the War of Independence led to the creation of the Irish Free State.

Women's franchise: Campaigns for women's full voting rights in national parliamentary elections began in the mid-nineteenth century. The National Society for Women's Suffrage was founded in 1872, the National Union of Women's Suffrage Societies in 1897 and the militant Women's Social and Political Union in 1903. Women over thirty who were householders or wives of householders, occupiers of property with an annual rent of £5 and graduates of British universities got the right to vote in 1918. Only in 1928 was this right given to all on equal terms.

Osborne House: A house on the Isle of Wight, built between 1845 and 1851 as a holiday retreat for Queen Victoria and Prince Albert, who drew up the designs himself. The Queen died there on 22 January 1901.

Page 93

Companion of the Order of the British Empire: This new order of chivalry was only established in 1917, so what is intended here is the Most Eminent Order of the Indian Empire, founded by Queen Victoria in 1878 under the title of Order of the Indian Empire as a reward for British and Indians who had served in India. In 1887 the more elaborate title was adopted.

Boers: From the Dutch/Afrikaans word for 'farmer', the term refers to the descendants of Dutch settlers in the eastern Cape, the Transvaal and Natal in South Africa. In the 1870s the British were expelled from the Transvaal. The Second Boer War, precipitated by the discovery of gold and diamonds in the Boer territories, lasted from 1899 to 1902, and eventually resulted in British victory.

Page 96

another famine in India: There was indeed a famine in 1896–97 over large parts of India, one of a sequence of famines in which millions died.

Pages 96–97

Kipling, 'The White Man's Burden': The poem was published in Britain and the United States in 1899. This phrase became a very popular means of conceiving Britain's belief in the 'civilizing mission' of her Empire, which was now being commended to America as a new imperial power.

Page 100

John Bull: A personification of Englishness, created for satirical purposes in the eighteenth century.

Page 104

'I closed my lids, and kept them close': From S.T. Coleridge, *The Rime of the Ancient Mariner* (see note to p. 15).